RAISING CAIN
(AND ABEL TOO)

The Parents' Book of
Sibling Rivalry

RAISING CAIN (AND ABEL TOO)

The Parents' Book of Sibling Rivalry

John F. McDermott, Jr., M.D.

Wyden Books

Manufactured in the United States of America.

FIRST EDITION

Designed by Tere LoPrete

Library of Congress Cataloging in Publication Data

McDermott, John F   1929-
    Raising Cain (and Abel too)

      1. Children—Management.   2. Sibling rivalry.   I. Title.
HQ772.M228   649'.143   79-66072
ISBN 0-87223-576-9

CONTENTS

ACKNOWLEDGMENTS: (*Thanks for More Than the Memory*)   xi

FOREWORD: *Two "Experts" at the Airport*   xiii

I. THE PROBLEM   3

Sibling Rivalry Is Normal, but . . .   3
. . . You Can and Should Influence It   7
So Don't Pretend It Isn't There   7
Is the Family a Democracy?   12
How Can You Teach Them to Share?   13
How Much Competition Should There Be?   16
Learning the Patterns—Who Does What to Whom?   22
The Sibling Checkup   23

II. THE CAUSES   27

Anyone Seen the American Family Lately?   27
Family Size—Large or Small?   30
How Many Children Should We Have?   35
Birth Order—Your Own   39
Don't Label Kids—They May Live Up to It   45
Sibling Position *Is* Important   49
    The Only Child   49
    The Firstborn   51

The Middle Child 57

The Youngest Child 59

When to Have the Second Child 61

Preparing for the New Baby 63

Why More Than One? 73

Parental Malpractice—Rejection and Preferences 75

Comparing Children to Each Other 78

Sex and Gender Preferences 82

Today's Changing Sex Roles 86

III. MANAGEMENT 90

Will They Outgrow It? 90

How Things Go Wrong 92

Are They Progressing or Regressing? 93

Phases of Sibling Relationships—An Overview of the Four Commandments 98

Might Equals Right 99

You Scratch My Back and I'll Scratch Yours 104

It's Not Fair, You're Cheating—The Law and Order Stage 108

As Brothers and Sisters Go, You're Not So Bad 117

A Conversation About Discipline and Sibling Rivalry—Handling Everyday Problems 120

Parental Problems with Discipline 126

Forms of Discipline to Use for Fighting 132

How Behavior Modification Works 143

Encouraging Kids to Communicate 145

When You Discuss Sibling Rivalry Directly 153

The Sibling Diary 154

The Instant Replay 157

Storytelling 159

Role Playing 161

The Family Map 163

Using the Paradox 167
Learning to Negotiate 170
Contracts and Problem Solving 173

IV. Special Situations 184

The Christmas Holidays 184
Birthdays and Birthday Parties 192
Games and Toys 198
Working Mothers 212
The Single-Parent Family 219

Conclusion—The Myths and the Realities 229
A Personal Postscript 239

To Sally,
Beth, and John
Who Made This Book Fun

ACKNOWLEDGMENTS

(Thanks for More Than the Memory)

First, I wish to express my gratitude to Peter Wyden, my publisher and editor. His ideas and suggestions were invaluable. He reoriented a child psychiatrist, accustomed to writing for scientific journals, to write this book as if it were a talk to a group of intelligent parents.

To the many psychiatrists and colleagues in the mental health professions with whom I have discussed the issues in this book over the years, I am indebted. There are too many to list individually. And to the mothers, especially Barb, Margie, Pat, and Dee, who shared experiences with their own children with me, I am most grateful. The children, parents, and teachers (especially Margaret and Pat) of the Children's Play School taught their consultant, Dr. Mac, more than they know about sibling rivalry. To Gail and Kathy who not only typed the manuscript but deciphered my impossible, scribbled changes, additions, and inserts, and served as the first audience for this book, I am indebted more than I can say. Their reactions as mothers of small children were a compass.

And finally, to my brothers, Marty and Ted, who introduced me to the subject in the nursery. I took the introductory course from them forty some years ago. Over the past fifteen years, I've been given the advanced course by my own children, Beth and John. During that time they both wittingly and unwittingly collaborated with me on this book. And finally to Sally, who, as usual, helped me understand it all.

FOREWORD

Two "Experts" at the Airport

One Saturday afternoon a few years ago, my psychiatrist friend and I were on our way to the airport in a large eastern city to catch a plane home. We were chatting about the child psychiatry meeting we'd attended over the past few days. After we checked in at the gate, we stopped off at one of those little gift shops so familiar in airports around the country—stocked with overpriced toys returning parents buy for their children, gladly paying a "guilt tax" for being away.

My friend, Fritz, was a well-known expert on child behavior and had written many books. We looked at the shelves of toys to pick out something for my five-year-old daughter and four-year-old son. It was as much fun trying out the toys as selecting.

"Hey, Jack, look at this windup monkey! It walks around and plays the cymbals! Johnny would like that. And here's a fur giraffe for Beth's animal collection."

"But, Fritz, what if *she* wants the monkey for her animal collection?"

Soon we were so worried about potential jealousy between the two kids that we found ourselves paying more attention to what each would *tolerate* as a gift for the other than to what each might have fun with. Our discussion got louder. We tried out more toys on the counter and in the aisle. The toot-toot-train whistled as it backed into the 747 with flashing lights. The saleswoman and some customers looked at each other as if we were crazy. Not appreciating we were "experts" in the field, they joined in our search, offering generous advice from their own experience.

"Get them both one of these puzzles—my kids always fight if they don't get the same present." (Good idea, but the puzzles were beyond my kids' level.)

"Naw, they got to be different—just get one blue and the other pink." (I wasn't sure my kids would know or care about the meaning of blue and pink.)

The security guard suggested pilot and stewardess wings or T-shirts that said Property of Alcatraz. An older couple watching said, "No, they need something that's fun to do, something they can play with."

A lady from Milwaukee suggested two different stuffed animals but added that her girls always looked at the other's gift first and said, "You can't win—they fight over everything anyway." A man from Los Angeles suggested the battery-operated remote control fire chief's car. It was expensive, so he said, "Get it for both of them to play with together." The saleswoman told him that five- and four-year-olds weren't old enough to share, particularly when they were excited. (I assume she meant Daddy coming home with presents.) She said, "Look at all those books on child development," pointing to the paperback stand, "none of them on when and why kids fight and what parents should do!"

She was right. Well-known books on raising children give sibling rivalry only passing reference. Many dismiss it by suggesting that if parents ignore fighting between brothers and sisters, they'll settle the conflicts themselves. Hardly.

Surveys and general impressions suggest that most parents feel they're doing a good job in raising their children. But they all express certain concerns. This book offers principles and suggestions aimed at the concern most frequently mentioned by all parents, those who feel they're doing a good job and those who don't. And that includes the lady from Milwaukee who asked why her children fight constantly and concluded that whatever you do "you can't win." She had given up too early. You can win!

Oh, I almost forgot. What did the "experts" in the airport finally decide? Two coloring books, slightly different from each other, each with a box of crayons, an experiment just to see if the kids were ready to accept something just a *little* different from each other. Luckily they did, and worked busily that evening comparing notes as they went along: "Look, I've got a fire truck" (bright green). "So what, I'm doing an ocean liner!" (bright red). They were happy.

And there's an extra dividend, too. Coloring books are not only biodegradable, they're psychodegradable. That is, they're consumable. Soon all the pictures are colored, scribbled, or passed over. Then there's nothing left to fight over. Until next time, that is.

RAISING CAIN
(AND ABEL TOO)
*The Parents' Book of
Sibling Rivalry*

I

THE PROBLEM

Sibling Rivalry Is Normal, but . . .

Remember Margaret Mead, the famous anthropologist? She was as well known for describing youngsters "coming of age" in America as in Samoa. Who could picture that wonderful woman, whose warmth, wisdom, and humor made her look like an ideal grandmother, slugging it out with her younger brother? But she did. Only when he deserved it, of course— for smashing a doll (or the latch to her door) with a hammer.* Sibling rivalry is normal and universal, but somehow parents don't believe it when it comes right down to their own children.

The Surgeon General Has Determined That Fighting May Be Hazardous to Their Health

It was a rainy day. Josh, age eight, and his brother Howard, six, were watching cartoons on television. Their mother was in the other room. She noted a danger signal—things were too quiet. Suddenly Howard said he didn't like the show and wanted to change the channel, which was against the house rule. So he began to poke Josh gently with his foot. Josh said, "Quit it!" Howard

---

* Margaret Mead, *Blackberry Winter* (New York: William Morrow and Co., 1972).

got in front of the TV so Josh couldn't see the picture. Josh shoved him aside. Zonk! Howard hit his head on the table. He screamed for his mother who came running.

Seeing Howard in tears, she scolded Josh. Josh shot back, "He started it." Mother said, "You're older and know better. Be nice to your little brother for a change!" Howard was smiling. Josh saw him. Mother left the room. Wham! Josh hit Howard with volume K-L of the children's encyclopedia.

"You're a spoiled brat," he shouted. "And if you squeal to Mommy you'll get it worse next time."

This time Mother had tried to be too understanding and expected more of Josh than he could handle, even as the oldest. But parents are resilient. And there's always going to be a next time. A few days later it happened again. She came in too late to know exactly what happened. So she said, "Boys, I'm sorry I didn't get here earlier so I don't know how it started. But either we all stick to the rule that someone can't change a program that's on without permission or off goes the TV!" For added emphasis, she sent both Josh and Howard to their rooms for a few minutes to break off the warfare.

Unfortunately, if there's one thing that temporarily blocks love and understanding for our children, it's fighting with each other. Maybe it brings back old memories and fears of fighting from our own childhood (if you were an only child, you probably can't understand it at all). Or maybe it's because we see our children as extensions of ourselves. When they hurt each other or get hurt, *we* feel it and get more angry and embarrassed than we need to. And that's why it always seems that *our* children fight more than others. Other kids seem to get along so well together. That's an illusion, too.

In any event, don't be afraid to intervene and don't feel guilty (or be made to feel guilty) about stopping it. Your kids don't have to like you all the time. It's more important to do what you think is right. If your innocent little Howard shouts from his room: "You hate me! You always put me up here in jail!" just think to yourself that all revolutionaries have to spend some time in jail reading and writing or they'd never have the credentials to lead a good revolution!

For that's what Howard is: a revolutionary. When there are two or more children in a family, there is—unfortunately, but inevitably—always some degree of rivalry. It's perfectly natural: a younger child usually envies the status and power of the older; the older is jealous of the younger child who isn't expected to do as much. Each feels the other is better off. Each struggles to be loved the most by the parents. It's the children's first experience in competitive living, and there can be no living without some degree of competition. Not as long as we're human.

But it can change from early bitterness into later friendship. Consider Golda Meir,* one of the greatest leaders in modern history, who devoted her adult life to the birth and rearing of the country of Israel. She was raised a Russian Jew under conditions of persecution, poverty, and hunger. She and her older sister fought all the time. When she really lost her temper, Golda would threaten to tell the neighborhood policeman all about Sheyna's political activities.

"I'll tell him that you and all your friends want to do away with the czar," she would shriek. It was a very real and powerful threat. It terrified Sheyna. Of course, it was classic blackmail—one way a younger child figures out to impress an older and stronger sister with her own importance. But Golda and Sheyna grew up to be closest friends. Sheyna was the one person whose praise and approval meant most to Golda when she was the leader of her country. Achievement had replaced threats as a more mature way to get recognition from her older sister.

* Golda Meir, *My Life* (New York: Dell Publishing Co., Inc., 1975).

If you think about it, a sibling relationship lasts a lifetime, longer than the parent-child relationship. In some parts of the world, it's considered the most important kinship tie, even more important than marriage or the one between parents and children. When brothers and sisters are three and four years old, they spend twice as much time together as they do with their parents. The difference increases as they get older. Competition between them can be a constructive experience and can strengthen a youngster for success in later life. Or it can continue on as a bitter battle toward everyone in life. You make the difference! And you *can* make a difference toward a constructive outcome. Want an example? Here's one.

When Wilbur and Orville Wright* were eleven and seven, their father brought home a single present for both of them. It was a toy "bat"—really a helicopter that flew with rubber bands. Naturally, they fought over such a fascinating toy, but their father didn't take it away. He encouraged them to study it and build better ones. Over the next few years, this challenge kept them together. They argued about the design for days on end. Because they thought they had to imitate a bird in order to fly, they argued about how the bird soars, how its wings are shaped when outstretched, and how it balances itself. They argued and argued. When one got an idea, the other soon thought up a better one. So it went, from one idea to another, building up like a pyramid.

Finally, on December 17, 1903, Orville climbed into a flying machine with an engine he and Wilbur had built together because no company would build it for them. He flew it for twelve seconds before an audience of five people. It was the first time in history a machine carrying a person had taken off and landed under its own power without being wrecked. It led to the jet plane that flies you across the country. And the driving

* Joseph Mersand (ed.), *Great American Short Biographies* (New York: Dell Publishing Co., Inc., 1966).

force was the rivalry between Wilbur and Orville, guided by their father so their energy was directed into a constructive rather than a destructive mixture of competition and cooperation. So don't despair when your little Wilbur and Orville are at each other's throat. There's hope!

. . . You Can and Should Influence It

Sibling rivalry has been with us since the human race began. Remember, the Bible records the first murder as a case of sibling rivalry—Cain, the firstborn, killing his brother Abel. The bloodiest wars in history have been civil wars, including our own in America, brother against brother.

It's your job as a parent to keep this natural rivalry under control as your youngsters mature and to help them channel it into healthy ways of getting ahead and getting along with others. I'll try to show you how, but a bit of patience helps, too. You can't instantly "teach" your children to love each other, and you can't simply stamp out rivalry between them. But you *can* influence it, especially if you view it as a universal part of development, not as a threat of total chaos. We know that it gradually decreases with age, given informed guidance.

Fighting between brothers and sisters is fierce in the first four or five years of life. Then, you must settle conflicts for them. Later you can help them settle disputes among themselves. Even later you can leave it up to them. But if you ignore the rivalry that comes with having two or more children, your kids may *stay* locked in battle with each other and even extend their hostilities to the outside world, to their relationships with others, as a way of life.

So Don't Pretend It Isn't There

They need your help. It's your job to act as a filter and a buffer between them. It's part of being a parent to deal with

it. Sometimes we like to think it's an extra burden, not part
of the job. Then we try to make it go away—just disappear—
or keep it from happening: "In *our* family, kids shouldn't
fight.

Let's see what happens when parents try to avoid the
issue and why they have an exaggerated fear of it in the
first place.

Eat Your Broccoli, It's Good for You

Mother and Father were busy talking over the dinner
table. The girls, Nancy and Kathy, were eating well, but
Dennis, always a picky eater, wouldn't touch his broccoli. It was the same every evening. Vegetables meant
war. Mother tried everything: coaxing, bribing, threatening—nothing worked. She finally reached the end of her
rope: "Please, honey, eat for *my* sake!" For Mother and
Father had agreed that they couldn't let Dennis get
away with not eating his broccoli. Everyone was equal
in the family, and if they let him off, it wouldn't be fair
to the girls. They might get upset, might accuse them of
favoritism, and probably would begin to refuse to eat
broccoli, too!

Father insisted, "Dennis, clean your plate!" Dennis
whined, "But, Dad, this stuff is yucky. It'll make me
throw up all over the table!" Father: "All right, then, go
to your room without dessert. Right this minute!" The
meal was spoiled for everyone. Mother was in tears.

Power struggles over food are notorious and dangerous mine
fields for parents. We seem to battle with youngsters over
food they don't like (broccoli) because it's good for them,
so we can then let them have what they like (dessert) that's
not so good for them!

In this case, Dennis winds up angry at his father, sitting in
his room planning to refuse to eat *whatever* is served the next

night. He's also furious at his sisters, because they were the "good" children. He'll get even with them, too! It would have been better if he'd been excused from the table early, so the struggle would have been shortened. The meal could have resumed pleasantly. The girls, if they cared at all, could be told that Dennis had likes and dislikes just as we all do and it's nothing to get excited about: "We're glad you girls like your vegetables so much."

The main point is: always start with an expectation that a youngster will eat, but don't be forced into a stronger and stronger response that becomes unreasonable and unworkable because it's too rigid. Don't stick to a policy when it becomes irrational. Letting Dennis off early is a price to pay to shorten the trouble time and restore a good atmosphere for the others. Everyone would have learned something from this.

Parents who go to any lengths to avoid any situation they're afraid will lead to fighting or arguing between brothers and sisters usually find that it boomerangs on them. They back themselves into a corner. Don't be afraid to treat children differently; they have different thresholds for likes and dislikes. Reducing the problem is different from avoiding it at all costs. Sibling rivalry is going to occur wherever children live in a family.

The myth that family members automatically love each other was shattered by Sigmund Freud as long ago as 1900 when he said: "Children are completely egoistic; they feel their needs intensely and strive ruthlessly to satisfy them . . . especially first and foremost against their brothers and sisters."* Alfred Adler, a follower of Freud who developed his own theory of personality development, based it entirely on the notion that our whole life as adults is preprogrammed by the competitive striving between siblings to "be first," that the basis of life is a power struggle starting in childhood.

While Adler's position may be extreme, the outcomes of

---

* Sigmund Freud, *The Interpretation of Dreams*, standard edition, volume 4 (London: Hogarth Press, 1953).

brother-sister struggles *are* important indicators of how young-sters will do in later life. Perhaps most important is the way parents respond. They are the key influences on children. There is no question: your children's relationships with each other must be faced as something more than a nuisance and annoyance. But how?

There are lots of things you can do. Some are simple, some more complicated. What parents first learn is that they can't stamp out fighting. It just flares up again. But if they can scale it down and keep it within reasonable bounds, they can *use* it to help their kids learn other ways, ways to live more peace-ably together. One of the best ways to start is to try to deflect their fighting, change it into something else. Here's an example.

Insanity Is Hereditary—You Get It from Your Kids

Mother was working at her desk. Little Susan and Freddie burst through the door rolling on the floor, arms and legs flailing in all directions. They shouted at each other: "He started it." "No, I didn't, she's a dirty liar. She took my candy bar and ate it all up." "Because he won't let me use his dart gun. He's the yuckiest, ugliest boy in the world!"

Mother: "You kids are driving me crazy. Every time I turn my back, you're trying to kill each other."

Mother was about to put them in their rooms. But she had an idea. Maybe she could defuse the fight and keep the two of them dealing with each other. Maybe that was better than just stamping it out. Because they might learn something from it. But both of them were too boil-ing mad inside to be able to do it themselves. She'd have to help.

Mother: "Come here, kids. I have an idea. You sit here, Freddie, and you sit there, Susan. Here's a big piece of drawing paper for each of you and some crayons. Let's see who can draw the ugliest picture of the other one."

What a chance! Hard to resist an offer like that. Both kids went to work. "Look at this face, Mommy—the nose is all smushed!" "Wait till you see this one—the beady eyes and the messy hair!"

The kids were breaking up with laughter. They'd forgotten all about the candy bar and the dart gun. They weren't that important anyway. The important thing was the way they felt about each other. Now they had a chance to show it without fighting. Mother had said it was okay.

Afterwards she saved the pictures. Drawing pictures probably wouldn't work next time, but next time she'd channel their rage at each other differently. She'd tape their pictures to the garage wall and let them shoot suction-tipped darts at each other's Ugly Picture. She knew this wasn't a real solution either. But it was a way of deflecting them away from physically attacking each other. She'd say to them, "Right now this is about the best I can think of. You kids seem to be so mad at each other all the time—so mad inside you can't handle it alone. So I've got to help. But I expect you to learn to control yourselves better and better. By talking it out— putting what you think about each other into words instead of pictures. Otherwise, it'll just go on and on and you'll never learn to live and let live."

Notice that Mother disapproved of the fighting but didn't take sides or blame one or the other. It was just one thing after another; who knows how it started? Now she got them to stop and move the fighting to a little higher plane. Not much higher, but a little. They went along. She made sure that the kids knew she wasn't approving of aggression in any form. They had to learn self-control as soon as they could. And ways of channeling their anger—better ways to settle things. Pictures and darts were just temporary. They helped deflect it into competition—an art contest, and later an art-gallery shooting contest. Better than slugging it out with fists, but only a temporary solution for young children. A permanent one gets more complicated. But this was a start.

Is the Family a Democracy?

Perhaps the most common basic confusion among parents today is whether or not the family is a democracy.

If they feel it should be, they tend to back off and avoid the role of mediator and referee. But to pretend the family is a democracy composed of equals suggests that a leader isn't needed. And to say that children will no longer accept parental authority just isn't true. Let's face it. The family is in fact a situation of unequal power. Unequal power among brothers and sisters is a principal reason for the fighting that goes on among them. Unequal power between children and parents is a means of controlling and channeling this rivalry if it is used responsibly. It's not a question of whether or not parents have authority, but how they use it and the efforts they make to help their youngsters grow up.

So, at best, the family is a guided democracy. For the way children are guided and learn to shift gears in dealing with each other, all the way from fighting to negotiation and finally to trust, is a crucial line of development. It goes a long way toward determining their success later in life, both in their work and in the relationships they'll create.

The ultimate responsibility for decisions that affect everyone's welfare is in fact with the parents, right? This should be made clear to the children. They'll be reassured if they know where they stand. And parents have another responsibility—to balance the development of each child as a separate person with a sense of family loyalty and connectedness. Family members need to stick together and support each other, sure, but they also need to grow away from each other and become different individuals. That's life. It's also a delicate and central issue. If you handle sibling rivalry well, you'll help each of your children to develop a special identity, a sense of who and what they are, their place in the family network.

How Can You Teach Them to Share?

The idea of group property and sharing, concepts parents would like to see from the beginning, emerges only gradually. Watch your young children playing in a sandbox. Their natural tendency is to play separately, alongside each other, during the second and third years. It's called parallel play. Whenever one child tries to interfere with the other's territory or equipment, wails of "That's mine!" erupt like a siren.

Gradually children learn to work together to build a bigger castle or dig a deeper hole and to pool their equipment—sand toys. It makes things more fun and gets more done. But they learn only by trial and error, by experiment and failure. By the age of four, they've realized that they can let a toy go, let someone borrow it, and it doesn't disappear forever. It usually comes back. If not, you know where to look to find it! But it's a process that takes several years. Don't think you can make it happen from the beginning by high-mindedness and sheer determination.

Beating Swords into Plowshares

The Lyons family believed in sharing. Everyone was equal. All for one and one for all. Anything that belonged to one member of the family belonged to them all. It was a firm principle and a good one. They believed that if it was adopted by the rest of the world, it might stop the fighting there, too. Their children, Nancy, five and a half, and Eddie, three, had complete access to each other's toys. Didn't it make sense that if you're trained from birth to share, you become a better person sooner?

Nancy's heroine was Princess Leia of *Star Wars*. All Nancy wanted for Christmas was the magnificent toy space station, Death Star, and the *Star Wars* action figures that went with it—especially Princess Leia. On Christmas morning there it was—under the tree. Nancy was bursting with excitement. But the card was a note from Santa. It said: "Please share this with your little brother."

Nancy knew that Eddie had his own toys and push toys were about all he was interested in. So she set about playing out the rescue scene starring Princess Leia. But the Death Star was just too much for little Eddie to resist. "I'm a tank," he shouted, and plowed into it. The tower broke. Wham! Nancy, in tears, socked Eddie, who ended up howling in pain. Both were sent to their rooms. The day was ruined.

The next day, Mrs. Lyons took the Death Star back to the department store to have it fixed. They told her it had to be sent to the factory. It would take several weeks. On the way home, she stopped off to see her friend, Jane. Over coffee, they talked about Christmas and she told Jane the sad story of Death Star.

Jane said, "What are you trying to do, raise your kids to live on a people's collective in the Ukraine? Why don't you read them the complete works of Marx and Lenin so they can really learn how to share? Eddie isn't old enough to play with a fancy toy like that one. He has his own things. Maybe there are some things they could share but you've got to pick 'em very carefully—and make sure they're indestructible! Not something special she's wanted so much for herself.

"Let me tell you, I learned early. I used to take my kids to the supermarket and every time they wanted some little thing, I said, 'Okay, if you promise to share it with your sister.' It was a sure way to get them to put it back—

not teach them how to share. It seemed to take all the fun and excitement out of things for a while.

"I began to realize that sharing has to come when they see it's the only way to deal with a problem—a problem that comes up naturally, like having only one banana left or only one swing at the playground. Then they're ready when you suggest taking turns. My kids have to share a room now, but they each have a private drawer. So some space they have to share, but some space is all their own. And the same goes for toys."

Mrs. Lyons: "But, Jane, I want them to grow up to be friends, to stick together and depend on each other."

Jane: "Don't you think that will come later? Right now, they're struggling to be *independent* from each other. Each of them, especially Nancy, wants to be a separate person. That's why they're fighting over being forced to share before they are ready. Maybe they need to prove they're *independent* from each other and can have things by themselves for a while. Then maybe they can volunteer to give up some of that precious individuality and share with each other. It's funny: the harder you try to get them to be close, the more they'll fight. The more you let them be different, the sooner they'll be friends."

Mrs. Lyons: "I guess maybe you're right. Maybe they need to be treated more like two separate kids. I've been making them eat the same things and putting them to bed at the same time because I wanted to treat them both the same. But it doesn't seem to be working out. They're more and more jealous of each other. Maybe if I do let them go different ways they'll begin to share when they begin to feel they won't be gobbled up by the other one."

Jane: "That's what I found with my kids. After you feel good about yourself, caring about others and sharing just naturally come along. Then it goes on from there—to

making truly close friendships like the one we have with
each other and the loving ones in marriage. When you
care as much about the other person's welfare as your
own."

Learning to take turns, to respect the wishes of others, and
to wait for your own wishes to be satisfied comes slowly, and
surprises parents pleasantly when they appear. When they do,
it's a reward for the patience and informed hard work of
raising children. But don't try to force them from the start.
In trying to push closeness, you may get the opposite results.
Instead, if you promote *separateness* (for example, mechanical
talent in one and musical talent in another) you'll find to
your amazement they'll become friends on their own. You
may not always be able to treat them equally, that is, all the
same, but you *can* try to treat them *fairly*. And that's not
only more important—it's also more attainable. A struggle
for independence goes on between brothers and sisters. It's
the stuff sibling rivalry is made of. You can actually minimize
it by helping them differentiate from each other, become
separate individuals. Then they don't have to *fight* so hard
to get that independence!

How Much Competition Should There Be?

Sibling rivalry is a kind of practice for life, something natural
that has to be kept under control, but neither to be avoided
nor to be overly encouraged by parents.

John F. Kennedy once said that he and his brothers soon
learned that competition in the family was a kind of dry run
for the world outside.* Everyone knows that the Kennedy
family was intensely competitive. House guests didn't survive
unless they played touch football with the same intensity.

* Victor Lasky, *JFK: The Man and the Myth* (New York: Dell Publishing
Company, Inc., 1963).

As Jack Kennedy's sister Eunice recalled, "The thing he [Daddy] always kept telling us was that coming in second was just no good. The important thing was to win—don't come in second or third, that doesn't count, but win, win, win!"

But that was for participating in the outside world. In the family, they were very close and actually *avoided* direct competition in serious matters. Seniority by age (and sex) was clearly to be respected. So the competition was softened with definite rules and roles, a pecking order with everyone deferring to the oldest sibling.

People marvel that the Kennedy boys each achieved such prominence. It seemed to be a succession. First Joe, Jr., then Jack, then Bobby, and now Ted. They all appeared to try to live up to the image of the older one as they remembered him. For example, whatever Joe did, Jack did next. Joe won all the championships at sailing; then Jack did. Then they became a team and won all the championships together.

"Just as I went into politics because Joe died," Jack Kennedy once said, "if anything happened to me tomorrow, my brother Bobby would run for my seat in the Senate. And if Bobby died, Teddy would take over for him." This was a powerful relationship between brothers, and it actually happened!

Betty Ford in her autobiography *The Times of My Life* sums up the clear boundaries youngsters place around rivalry. She recalled how her sons gave their sister a hard time. "She used to come down to breakfast dressed for school. The night before, she laid out her clothes carefully: dress, shoes, the right color ankle socks to match the outfit. She'd get to the table and they'd start. 'Ow, it hurts my eyes!' 'Boy, what an ugly skirt.' 'You're not going to wear *that*, are you?' She looked darling but they never quit criticizing. Which didn't mean they'd let an outsider do the same. It was okay for them to pick on her, but a stranger had better not try it."*

Let's look at how delicate an issue competition is. In the

* Betty Ford, *The Times of My Life* (New York: Harper and Row, 1978).

right amount, it prepares children for life, for achievement and success. If overdone, it can destroy their chances or make them successful but unable to be happy or enjoy it.

Nice Guys Finish Last

Joe Adams was a class A tennis player. He was determined that his youngsters, Ann and Paul, would be the same. They were moving up in their age groups. Each weekend he practiced with them. "Don't let up, Ann, you've got him 40-love! Murder him!" "Okay, Paul, she's moved up to the net. Now crank it! Aim for her head. That's the way to keep them away from the net."

Paul: "But, Dad, I don't want to. Can't I just aim for her chest?" Joe: "That's the trouble, you don't have the killer instinct! You're never going to be number one that way."

Joe Adams couldn't understand why his youngsters did so well in tennis but were called "ding-dongs" by their classmates. They had no friends. They cried when they lost and seemed under enormous tension. Paul often threw his racket when he lost a point. He swore loudly at himself. It was as if he carried his father's criticism around with him. Ann learned to hit it "down their throats" but couldn't play doubles with her brother. They should have been the best mixed doubles team in the state, but they constantly fought, claiming the other had made a mistake that lost the point or the match. Each was trying hard to please their father, but at the other's expense, so teamwork was impossible. Each took shots away from the other.

Fortunately, Paul and Ann's mother saw some of their matches and saw the need to lessen the tension. She saw that each was trying to be better than the other and that both were losing ground because they were terrified of failing. She began asking them, "Did you have a good game?" rather than "Did you win?" Then she asked what they learned from a match, what shots they felt the best about and which ones they wanted to improve. Fortunately, Joe also began to worry about the problems that might be coming between the two youngsters from his emphasis on one beating the other.

Mother: "Didn't I hear that the Olympic idea of 'taking part' is as important as winning—doing your best? If we left the kids to their own devices, they'd probably take up sports just to make friends and to have fun. We're the ones who put the emphasis on winning, not them. They'd simply want to be a member of the tennis team. That's the way kids look at it. But we seem to push competition and not the give-and-take and just plain enjoyment of playing."

Joe: "Maybe I've put on too much pressure to win and I should really work on getting them to work to their potential. I've been ignoring them or giving them the silent treatment when they lose. Maybe I should let them know that losing is painful but it isn't the end of the world. You play again tomorrow or next week and you aren't a personal failure."

Mother: "And just because someone has to win and someone has to lose, no matter how close the match is, doesn't take away the fact that the loser might have worked just as hard as the winner."

Joe: "Yeah, that's right. I'm beginning to realize that trying to pick up or develop a skill while you're under the gun to win must be awfully hard. I've been expecting that of them, so they've been losing self-confidence rather than gaining it."

Parents can unwittingly promote rivalry and competition between their youngsters beyond the normal range in which it will occur anyway. It then becomes destructive and self-defeating, continues on beyond childhood, and interferes with achievement and performance by its very intensity.

It's said that learning a sport goes through several stages.* The beginner is trying to acquire the basic technique and the new kind of muscular coordination which seems complicated and difficult. It's fun at this stage because you are learning something new and that is a reward in itself. You don't *have* to win because no one expects you to yet. It's just fun meeting new people and doing new things. When you get better, you get a sense of pride in competing with other people and while you may not win against more experienced players, you figure that you will if given more time. But the ability to play well is still more important than the need to win.

Ron Guidry, ace pitcher for the New York Yankees and one of the best baseball pitchers of the 1970s, has stayed at this level. He says, "The only thing I could improve on is to pitch better—not win more games, but pitch better. There were some games [in 1978 when he won twenty-five games] where I struggled and got the same results." His philosophy is to improve himself, not simply beat the other team. He knows that many of his wins are lucky.

When the better players have played well for some time, they may become totally committed to the sport and must win to enjoy it. They feel miserable if they lose. You don't need to condemn them. They do it themselves. Arguments develop, because beating somebody else is the only new satisfaction. But they don't have to reach this stage. Indeed, it's hardly a stage of progress. It's really a step backward into the world of smaller children, of jealousy, where it's not just the need to win but the need to *beat* others to feel good. Parenting makes the difference between remaining a jealous child or growing up.

* Sid Sackson, *Beyond Competition* (New York: Pantheon Books, Random House, 1977).

Joan Fontaine in her autobiography *No Bed of Roses* describes the competition with her equally famous movie actress sister, Olivia de Havilland. Both were successful. Both won Academy Awards. But in 1941, when *both* were nominated for the Best Actress Award and Ginger Rogers announced the winner as Joan Fontaine, Joan says, "I froze. I stared across the table, where Olivia was sitting directly opposite me. 'Get up there. Get up there,' she whispered commandingly. Now what had I done! All the animus we'd felt toward each other as children, the hair pulling, the savage wrestling matches, the time Olivia fractured my collarbone, all came rushing back in kaleidoscopic imagery.

"My paralysis was total. I felt Olivia would spring across the table and grab me by the hair. I felt age four, being confronted by my older sister. Damn it, I'd incurred her wrath again!"

Joan Fontaine ends her book with a plea to her mother: "I never knew why you didn't try to make us kinder, more understanding, more forgiving of one another—or did you prefer us at each other's throat?"*

Shirley MacLaine and her brother Warren Beatty, the famous actress and actor-director, also had competition pressed on them by their family, but it was handled differently. "Warren and I were allies. We had to be, otherwise we found ourselves battling each other, vying for favor as a result of competition imposed on us by our parents. They probably didn't even know they were doing it but Warren and I felt it. We would fight each other until an outside force intruded. Then we stuck together."†

You can see them stick together today. They call each other often and Shirley says that Warren looks for girl friends like her.

---

* Joan Fontaine, *No Bed of Roses* (New York: William Morrow & Co., 1978).
† Shirley MacLaine, *Don't Fall Off the Mountain* (New York: W. W. Norton and Company, 1970).

Learning the Patterns—Who Does What to Whom

Who Dunnit? Nobody Knows the Trouble I've Seen

The kitchen was a mess. Lucy, seven, Mark, five, and Cindy, three, had been eating lunch. Mother heard the giggling, then the shouts, then the crash. When she reached the kitchen, food was all over the room. The milk pitcher was shattered and milk was all over the floor. The children were shouting and crying. "Who did this?" asked Mother rhetorically. The usual chorus responded, "She did." "He did." "She did." "All right, if I can't find out who started it, you'll go to your rooms for the afternoon!" Mother angrily cleaned up the kitchen, helped by an uninvited assistant, Kissinger, the family dog.

There was probably no way to find out who started the food fight. The children themselves didn't know, so how could they tell their mother? Why shouldn't they blame each other? Mother asked them in such a way that the answer was inevitable. It really was a piece of joint mischief; the high excitement level produced the contagion needed to involve everyone. Punishing everyone will lead to reconstruction of the event instead of forgetting it, with more claims of individual innocence and blame on the others.

What to do? Mother might well have had all the children clean up the kitchen together. It would have gone slowly; she could do it herself faster. But by reducing guilt in the children (actually their labor scrubbing the floor would allow Mother to save face and be able to forgive them, which is the important thing), Mother could have prevented a further buildup of rivalry. Training the children to blame "the other guy" and to squeal without thinking is the last thing she wants.

This lesson—when things get out of hand and mischief becomes contagious, then everyone has to pitch in and patch things up—is more important than the one Mother chose, that the guilty party must be identified.

Well, you may ask, why should everyone have to suffer by going to their rooms *or* cleaning up together? Shouldn't parents encourage individual responsibility? One shouldn't suffer for the other's crime.

Yes, that's true *if* you can identify the cause. Lots of the time you can't. Besides, there is a need for a balance. Each child needs to learn about being responsible for himself/herself, *and* for all, too. So don't feel you have to deal with the individual *all* the time. Try to discover repetitious happenings, the patterns and general relationship of each of your children to the other. This will give you a better idea of problems between them.

Here's how to find out.

The Sibling Checkup

When you take the children to the pediatrician for a checkup, he measures them. He checks their height, weight, size of the head, watches the movement of their eyes, looks in their throat and ears, listens to their heart and lungs, feels their abdomen, checks their reflexes, takes their pulse and blood pressure. He then adds up all the findings and measurements and places your youngster on a spectrum between health and illness.

You can do the same kind of checkup for patterns of sibling relationships. If you do this periodically, you will not only note changes and be able to respond to them, but you will identify patterns, problem areas, and potentially dangerous situations so you can then arrange to minimize them or at least be present to supervise. For example, Mark, Lucy, and Cindy aren't yet able to eat together. Perhaps two of them can, but the three of them need supervision if they're to have lunch together. If you watch at lunch you can tell how collisions begin.

Count the number of fights. Note what they're about; e.g., parental attention, possessions, physical space, games, etc. Also note the times when things go well. In school age children, if fighting occurs almost all of the time they're together and they seem unhappy much more of the time than they are happy, this may signal a problem that goes beyond "normal" sibling rivalry. Listen and watch at meals to see the percentage of reasonably pleasant discussions versus arguments and disagreements.

Watch TV with them and ask them questions about the programs. They will share their view of the world with you if you try to see things through their eyes and minds rather than just your own.

Give them a task to do together, simple and short for young children and perhaps a little more complicated for older ones, such as chores around the house. Or watch them playing a game together.

Keep in mind: the kind of game they're playing will tend to heighten or diminish the competitiveness of the situation. Still, you can observe how they work out differences. With youngsters of different ages and different skill levels, it's obviously important to try to even things out so that one is not always losing and one winning, either by giving the more experienced and skilled one a handicap or by choosing a game in which luck counts more than skill. (See the section "Games and Toys" in Chapter IV.)

Perhaps most important is learning how to communicate with your children *between* fights, not during or after them when you and they are likely to be angry, frustrated, and therefore less likely to flush out what's really going on. Ask them from time to time what each likes best (and least) about the other. If you get an answer like "He follows me around and imitates my best friend and calls her fat!" you'll know what deserves your attention—jealousy of having a best friend. Here are some other parent-child dialogues I've heard:

"When do you fight the most?"

"When one of us feels you or Dad are being unfair or that you're playing favorites. You probably don't even know you were doing it or why we're fighting."

"How does your brother get you to do what he wants?"

"Well, if he did something for me, and he says now it's my turn to do something for him, I'm caught. I have to help with the dishes when it's his turn."

"How do you get your sister to do what you want her to do?"

"Well, sometimes I talk her into playing with me or sometimes I'll offer a favor like letting her play with my hamster. Sometimes I even tickle her and then she gives in."

"What do you kids like to do together that's fun?"

"Well, going to the store on our bikes and sometimes going to a movie if it's the kind of movie we both like."

"What's the worst thing Charley ever did to you, Emily?"

"He took my doll and broke it because I went into his room and just *touched* his radio-controlled flying saucer!"

"How about you, Charley?"

"She always wants to watch some dumb cartoon when 'Star Trek' is on, and when I try to change the channel, she scratches me. Once she even made me bleed!"

Put yourself in their shoes and try to figure out where they stand when they deal with each other. What's their particular value system? Where are they most sensitive? What bugs them the most that the other does?

You'll be surprised to discover that brothers and sisters often have their own rules for getting along, just as husbands and wives do in marriage—rules that tell them how far each can go. They're working out conflicts behind the scenes. You need to know which level of negotiation skills they have achieved so you can deal with them in a way they will understand and that will therefore be effective. (See the sections on communication and negotiation in Chapter III.)

In sibling rivalry the spectrum between normal and abnormal is just like the one between health and illness that your pediatrician uses. Normality occupies over 90 percent of the spectrum. But if one youngster is constantly being beaten up, fighting is virtually nonstop and extends beyond the sibling relationship to problems with peers in the neighborhood, at school, with authorities outside the family (such as teachers), these may be warning signs of an "illness" pattern. These are signs that normal sibling rivalry has become extreme and excessive. Then it may need professional assessment so it doesn't become fixed and part of a lifelong pattern.

II

THE CAUSES

Anyone Seen the American Family Lately?

Certainly everyone is aware of the dramatic change in the structure and function of the family over the past two decades. It's no longer as child oriented or even as family oriented as it once was. It's more individually oriented—the wishes of the individual (the "I" or "me" society) are a predominant force pushing toward fragmentation of the family.

From large families we have moved toward smaller families with fewer and fewer children. While in previous generations there was often an oldest child, several middle children, and a youngest, now two-children families have become typical. So there are more "oldest" and "youngest" growing up next to each other without the buffer of middle children. These smaller families are often headed by an overinvolved mother and a father who is isolated from the rest of the family and separates himself, making cohesion even more difficult. And the one-parent family has become a statistical norm. Necessarily the single working parent caring for several children is particularly harassed as the kids become increasingly competitive for a smaller amount of available parental nurturance. (See the section "The Single-Parent Family" in Chapter IV.)

For Better, For Worse

Frank and Barbara Stevens have two children, aged five and three. Frank is a hardworking accountant in a large corporation. The family has moved twice in the last two years. Frank is moving up. He works long hours and is rarely home for dinner.

Barbara is at the end of her rope with the children. They fight constantly over toys and for her attention. Frank has a short temper and spanks them when things get too loud. He never has fun with the children and hardly knows them. Barbara thinks often of divorce and has little energy left for her youngsters. She develops a "front parlor" philosophy throughout the house: *every* room must be perfectly clean and neat as if it's only used when company comes. The children begin to sneak food into the TV room.

Barbara has little or no support from Frank either to refuel her with needed affection or to share the job of parenting. She begins to feel totally helpless with the children; she must have *something* she can keep under control, otherwise she feels she'll go crazy. So the house becomes an obsession. She thinks she ought to be able to control the house; it's not human like the kids. But several young children make that way of coping, keeping a perfect house, very difficult. The kids just can't wear their emotional tuxedos and evening gowns and be on their tidiest behavior all day long. They also feel the tension in their mommy.

They begin to fight with each other more because there is so much pressure to behave. It's as if they were in Sunday school all week at home. And Mother is less available to them; she is so obsessed with her house that it resembles an art museum with Do Not Touch signs on everything.

The children are angry, but they can only take it out on each other. If only Frank and Barbara were able to sit down and review their marriage they'd find that the children's increased fighting is a symptom of its breakdown. The parents are not fighting; the children are doing it for

them. They even fight over who is the messiest and who
is boss. If Frank would listen to Barbara's problems and
help her as a partner in caring for the children by being
home at critical family times (such as dinner time), the
kids' fighting would slow down.

Frank and Barbara need to discuss or write down a list
of what each expects from the marriage (beyond the for-
mal marriage contract) and in what ways each feels let
down and has let down the other. They can do this themselves without professional help if they decide to. Otherwise, the progession toward divorce seems inevitable. And
Barbara, who would most likely have custody of the children, will feel even more helpless and angry.

Fortunately, this couple decided to take a vacation together and began to work things out, Barbara realizing
how possessive of the children she was for the first few
years, which helped to cause Frank's sense of loneliness
and isolation, a feeling he can now acknowledge. When
they got home, they made up a new set of rules together.
Barbara said to the kids, "You don't have to sneak food in
the TV room anymore. It's okay to eat in there as long as
it isn't the crumbly or sticky stuff." The children: "Great,
Mom, but do we always have to go outside to play?" Barbara: "You guys do need a place in the house to play
rough-and-tumble. Let's make a playroom in the base-
ment. Okay?" The children: "Sure. But can we play in
the living room if we promise to be good?" Barbara:
"Well, it's awfully hard to play in the living room and not
knock things over. Every room has a different purpose.
The game room will be for play, the living room is for
quiet things, like looking at picture books." The children:
"Okay, Mommy, that can be your game room."

Frank and Barbara began to negotiate a closer relationship.
The disagreements and quarrels abated. The cold war had
ended. The children began to fight less, partly because they

were under less pressure and partly because they could see a more natural give-and-take between their parents. Secretly, they had known of the tension between Frank and Barbara. Like all kids, they were curious about their parents and noticed when there was a strain between them and problems that weren't solved. But of course they couldn't *say* anything. Children are to be seen and not heard. But ask any child, even a three- or four-year-old, and you can find out what the relationship between their parents is like.

Now that they began to see problems arise and get solved instead of going underground and ending up in *their* fights, the kids no longer had to fight the *parents'* battles.

Family Size—Large or Small?

For years people idealized a television family as a model: the Waltons. It was a large family, poor but dignified, with strong loyalties and many flexible and healthy ties so that when one member was in trouble, the others came to the rescue. Rivalries were present but soft. The family worked and lived around common interests and jobs, i.e., the family farm and sawmill. Most of us in the television audience have imagined ourselves one of the Waltons and privately yearned for such a family of our own, with the several generations living smoothly together.

The special appeal of that program is interesting in the face of the realities of present-day America with an "average" family of parents and two children, the "minimum" family reduced to one parent and one child, and the overstressed one-parent family becoming more and more common. Watching some television shows, especially those in which relationships between members of the family are idealized, may make you feel worse about your own. On television, problems are solved in thirty or sixty minutes! There isn't the daily confusion and conflict of real families, where problems go on and on, finally resolved in so many ways, often not completely as you had hoped, rarely ideal.

In reality, large families have their problems, too. They're not sounder or happier because they're larger. Let's consider some of the problems among children in large families today.

Our Children Always Come First

George and Sally always wanted a large family because neither had come from one. George was an only child and Sally the youngest of two. So they had six children and took pride that in any decision affecting the family, the children came first. They often sacrificed vacations, new clothes, and gave up a second car for the children. A youngster's wish, particularly a young child's wish, invariably became the focus for the family's concern and attention. Bedtime was chaos. All the children went to bed at one time and fought for songs and stories.

"He gets more than I do" was the cry.

Soon George and Sally began to wonder why their children didn't seem to be growing up. More and more fights broke out between them. Charley, age ten, Thomas, age nine, and Joan, age seven, were all acting like babies instead of school age children. They screamed and pounded when they wanted something. They were highly jealous. If one did well in school, he was bound to be picked on. No one tolerated anyone else getting ahead, even outside the family.

In this family, "children always come first" meant that one had to act like a young child to get one's needs met. A child was a child. There was no recognition of differences between them as they grew older and different from each other. So it didn't pay to act older. Everyone was rivalrous with everyone else and fought ferociously for crumbs of affection from the parents who had little or no experience growing up with other children. The parents were at the end of their rope.

If George and Sally could realize that an increase of responsibility with age must be presented to the kids as an advantage, not a disadvantage, they could reverse this pattern which was so frustrating to everyone. Bedtimes should be staggered by age. Being little and helpless should not be the most prized position. Everyone should be himself or herself. Differences between the children should be openly acknowledged so they would not all act alike or decide to stay little and for good reason: it was not only safe there but that was how their parents seemed to care most for them.

In most larger families youngsters fortunately help socialize each other. They teach each other fair play, self-control, sharing, to listen as well as to talk. A good deal of the intensity of jealousy and rivalry between children is diluted and spread around by sheer numbers. Often two "sets" of siblings evolve—the older group who are developing interests outside the home and the younger set, still involved in getting love from parents and each other, becoming socialized at home before going out in the world to join their older brothers and sisters. And mixtures occur. Rose Kennedy describes her son Teddy, the youngest in a large family, as having more time with his father than the others. But Ted recalls that his brother Jack, who was older by fourteen years, was a combination father and brother to him. Given this mixture, he was "more approachable and better able to look at the lighter side of situations."*

Other children are often assigned (or assume) a parenting role for the younger ones, and while this has some advantages because the children can teach each other and look out for each other, this triggers problems, too. A twelve-year-old may be able to feed the baby but may do it in a mechanical fashion, without the physical closeness so important in the nursing experience. A ten-year-old can take charge of the younger ones but does not

* Rose Kennedy, *Times to Remember* (New York: Doubleday, 1974).

have the maturity to be a parent and often takes advantage of them. (See the section "The Firstborn" in this chapter.)

Often the youngsters split off into pairs that reflect similar interests or talents—for example, sports or playing musical instruments. The intensity of friction is usually greatest between two adjacent siblings. Alternate siblings, the first and third, the second and fourth, often form a coalition against their common rival in the middle. So the middle one gets a double dose—he/she gets it from both sides. Parents need to be aware of this pattern because it will often predict where the source of fighting and friction is located among brothers and sisters.

How to Become a Spoiled Brat

Susie, age six, complained constantly that her sisters, Ann and Chris, two years older and younger, respectively, were picking on her, stealing her toys, playing tricks, scaring and teasing her. One day she came crying to Mother, "They let the air out of my tires." The bike was a new two-wheeler she was learning to ride and had been a birthday present. Mother tried to console her. "Here, Susie, here's a quarter for ice cream. I'm going to the store anyway. Why don't you come along?" Ann and Chris were watching every move. When they saw this, they began to plot how they could catch Susie and lock her in the attic. "We'll get that spoiled brat," said Chris, clenching her teeth in rage.

It's easy to feel sorry for Susie. But it might have been wiser for Mother, instead of indulging Susie on impulse, thereby fueling the jealousies further, to talk to all three girls about the problem: "You know, girls, there's always a tendency for two to gang up against one. It's natural, especially when they feel that one is the favorite. But it must be especially hard for Susie, too. She's a younger sister to you, Ann, and an older sister to you, Chris. So each of you have a different reason not to like her. Chris, you and Ann have your differences too. But you seem to avoid fights between yourselves by joining forces against Susie."

If, instead of a special treat for Susie, Mother could casually take *all three* for ice cream in the next day or so, it might be a good chance to talk things over. The hidden resentments about favoritism might begin to become less intense. At least they wouldn't be reinforced.

The smaller and smaller families encouraged throughout the world today by the universally declining birthrate make it even more important for us to stand back, understand, and influence sibling relationships. You have ways to make up for (and to provide the opportunities for) growth that were available in the larger families more typical of years past. You can direct more effort toward frequent discussions about how members of the family are getting along with each other and present "hypothetical" problem-solving situations. These make up for the absence of natural chances to learn to work out incidents between a larger number of brothers and sisters.

Mother:	"What if there's a house with one television set and everyone wants to watch their own favorite programs? What should the people do?"
John, six:	"No one can watch unless everyone agrees."
Mother:	"But everyone is different and likes different things."
Mary, eight:	"The oldest gets the first choice."
Mother:	"But that's not fair either. Joey would never get to watch his favorite cartoons."
Joey, five:	"No one can watch!"
John:	"You have to reserve it in advance."
Mary:	"That just leads to more fights."
John:	"Well, reserve it for specials then."

Mary:	"How about this: whoever is watching has firsts and the program can't be changed without permission?"
Joey:	"Okay. I get to watch tonight 'cause you have homework and I'm too little."
Mary:	"Why don't we say no television on school nights and get one of those things that records programs so we could save real good ones for the weekends?"
Mother:	"We'll see. Anyhow, you kids are really getting somewhere working things out. I guess rules work much better if everyone has a say-so when they're being made."
John:	"Oh yeah? Well, where's Dad? *He* decides about sports programs without asking *anyone!*"
Mother (laughing):	"Let's continue this when he gets home."

How Many Children Should We Have?

Of course no can decide for you. It depends on so many factors. Twenty years ago the typical newly married couple hoped to have four or five children. Today they may plan for one or two. Something has happened to cause families to grow so much smaller in this relatively short time.

The large number of smaller families seems to be based on economics. A couple decides how many children they can afford because they want to provide the best things for their children. If, for example, they want them all to go to college, the number has to be limited. Selecting certain ones who can go, often the oldest with the others staying home, is no longer considered fair.

Actually economics has always been a major factor in determining family size. The large families of years gone by were necessary because children died early from diseases that can now be controlled. Parents had a larger number of children, figuring that about half of them would survive past early childhood. Frequent illnesses and deaths in the family were a source of concern to everyone and held it together.

Years ago children were prized as workers who could contribute to the family's income early in life. They grew up quickly, too quickly, into "little adults," often exploited by grown-ups, not valued for themselves. If rivalries occurred between them, they were often over matters of sheer survival. There was literally no period called adolescence. Adolescence is a new phenomenon, a period when education can be extended through high school and college.

Another factor affecting the changing size of families needs to be considered by parents when they decide how many children to have: when to have them. This decision itself is relatively new—the era of modern family planning. Most parents of young children have lived when improved contraceptive methods have allowed them not only to choose how many children to have, but even when to have them and how far apart to space them. Now, when it's more common for both parents to work, these become very important decisions which can be controlled.

Parents can decide just how much they have to "give" to children in an emotional sense, and this helps determine how many children they decide to have. Of course in reality it's not so easy to predict how many children would be "right" for you. Today many couples are deciding not to have children at all because they don't want the responsibility. This is a perfectly reasonable decision. Not everyone should have children—only those who want them and have plenty of love and affection to give them. The unwanted child is at high risk for all kinds of problems.

Also the trend toward an "I" or "me" philosophy brings people together for transient relationships, for immediate satisfactions rather than lasting closeness. Unfortunately they usually don't find happiness in a continual search for pleasure; the greatest happiness is found in relationships with others, particularly intimate relationships with a spouse and children who are felt as a part of one's self.

Rolling Stones Gather No Moss

Robbie and Andrea were children of the sixties who had been living together for a year and a half. Both agreed that self-actualization and self-realization were the ultimate goals they shared in common. But one day Andrea found herself pregnant. Her immediate thought was to have an abortion, but she wondered whether this was the time for her and Robbie to consider marriage and start a family. Robbie replied, "Look, I'm on my trip and you're on yours. If you want to join me on mine, fine. If you don't, go bleep yourself!"

Andrea seems to be experiencing the need for someone else. Rather than self-centeredness, she is wondering about motherhood and mutuality. But Robbie makes it clear that, at least at this point in his life, he has no love left for anyone besides himself. It's probably best they not have a child, certainly not several. Some people do not really have enough love to give to children. That's why some marriages are quite stable until children arrive; after that they "destabilize" with more and more conflict. Some have enough love and patience to give to one child; others two or three. Some people have enough of what used to be called "mothering," now called "parenting," ability, so they have the capacity for raising a number of children well.

If you've decided to have children, it's probably best, if you can, to have more than one. An only child is likely to be lonely. That doesn't mean he or she can't grow up healthy and happy. But it is harder. (See the section "The Only Child" in this chapter.) Life may seem quieter for parents without the sibling rivalry of two or more to grapple with, but two children work things out, sharpening their personalities against each other as they grow up. This gives them an advantage in maturity.

There's an often crucial counterpoint: parents usually don't anticipate the intensity of normal rivalry. They want and expect children who are happy and love each other. They want peace and harmony in the family. They may feel lost or betrayed by what seems almost constant fighting. Sometimes they wish they'd stopped with one child. When the fussing-fighting-feuding stage is outgrown (see the section "Will They Outgrow It?" in Chapter III) they are equally surprised ("I thought it would never stop") and can appreciate the advantages of having a brother or sister. They have a head start in the outside world—a variety of methods for dealing with others. In sports and other activities requiring teamwork, for example, they're generally better team players than children who have no brothers or sisters.

Many satisfactions await parents when they have a second child. They are generally much less worried and concerned than about the first. Like the only child, the firstborn has a special relationship with the parents. He or she is their first experiment in parenting. It's been said that the firstborn brings up the parents. But now things can be more relaxed and fun. You don't have to prove anymore to everyone (including yourself) that you can be a parent. It's as if you buy your first car just after learning to drive. You'll be somewhat tense and worried, even awkward and clumsy with that car. As the months go by, you become more experienced and skilled. When you're ready to buy your next car, you'll drive it with much more skill and be considerably less nervous. It's a matter of getting used to a role, being a driver.

But how far apart? Parents with children very close in age, one to two years apart, report more intense fighting between them than those further apart.

Jimmy Carter in his autobiography *Why Not the Best?* related many of his problems as a child to his sister Gloria who was one year younger. He recalled Gloria hitting him with a wrench, shooting her with a BB gun, and Gloria getting him punished by their father. It seemed easier for him to be a respected big brother to the younger siblings. Gloria was just too close.*

Does that mean children should be spaced far apart? Not necessarily. If they're five or six years apart, they will be more like separate single children, not quite "only children." At first, the older may be more intensely jealous of the new baby because he/she is more aware of it. A four-year-old might say inside, "Why did they have to bring this little monster into the house? Wasn't I good enough? Why did they want another one?" And the oldest will be jealous. The baby will seem spoiled and given all the attention. The baby is a bitter rival, no question. Over time, the age difference is an advantage. They develop different sets of friends and a natural independence from each other. They have less effect on each other than those who are closer in age and spend more time together.

Two and a half to three and a half is probably the best age difference if you want to avoid these extremes and still give your children the experience of being brothers and sisters, which can lead to a closeness that lasts throughout life. You may not believe it now, but it happens.

Birth Order—Your Own

What about the order in which children are born into a family? How does it affect them and family life to be the first, second, or third born?

First, an even more basic consideration: how *our own* birth order affects us for life and is unwittingly transmitted into the way we bring up our children.† It's our hidden family tree.

---

* Jimmy Carter, *Why Not the Best?* (New York: Bantam Books, 1975).
† Walter Toman, *Family Constellation* (New York: Springer Publishing Company, Inc., 1969).

Even though family size and structure may have changed over the past generation, our *own* personal family background continues to live in the present and influences us as parents. Our experience in our family of the past just doesn't disappear when we grow up and leave home. It is part of our makeup. And sometimes this can cause problems in our family of the present, especially if we remain unaware that *we* may be the source of the problems, not the children.

The Way We Were

Marge and Bill Fox were continually fighting over who was boss of the house. They agreed on very little. Discipline for the children was inconsistent. Favoritism led to Marge lining up with their son against Bill. Bill sided with their daughter against Marge. Breaking up the husband-wife combination and reshaping it into parent-child alliances is always a clear danger sign. The warfare over who was boss intensified.

Neither Bill nor Marge could understand how their best friends, Alice and Jerry, got along so well. Alice and Jerry seemed to work together as parents; they divided up roles, with Alice taking a somewhat stronger one. Their other close friends, Tom and Joan, also got along well in managing their four children, Tom seeming somewhat more in charge. But, as with Alice and Jerry, mutual decision making was the principal way of operating.

The decisive factor in these families had nothing to do with differences between a man's role and a woman's. As we all know, there's more and more blurring of the traditional differences between male and female roles because the concept of equality between the sexes is filtering into parenting. In this case, the problem was a matter of *sibling position repeating itself.*

Marge and Bill had both been the oldest children in their

families. As the eldest, each had lots of responsibility and had assumed leadership. If you asked their brothers and sisters, there was no question who was in charge. Having come together in marriage from dominant roles, they found it hard to agree on anything because each wanted to be in charge and have the final say. They even became rivals over who was organizing a family picnic. No wonder: "being in charge of the children" and the children's activities was a right each had held exclusively in the formative years of their lives.

Alice and Jerry, by contrast, grew up in families in which Alice was the oldest girl with several younger brothers, and Jerry was the youngest, a boy with two older sisters. They were able to "fit" together and complement each other rather than compete because they found in each other the match they were used to earlier. Alice took a somewhat more decisive role when the chips were down, which was quite agreeable as a family style for Jerry. He was used to it; he had looked up to his older sisters as he was growing up.

Tom and Joan had come from the opposite family configuration. Tom had been the oldest brother; Joan was the youngest sister who looked up to her older brothers. In marriage, this enabled them to look to each other with respect, not competition; their accustomed relationship to the opposite sex was partially replicated in their marriage.

Not that successful or unsuccessful marriages are based on previous sibling position. But it is one factor and sometimes an important one. The accident of birth order produces a kind of "pseudoheredity" that we usually overlook completely.

Take a look at your own family background, position in the family, and relationship to your brothers and sisters. Then compare that with your spouse's. Old feelings toward yourself and your brothers and sisters continue throughout life. They can be reactivated in new situations, particularly when personal problems of everyday living together must be worked out once again.

Marge and Bill Fox were comfortable with the opposite sex

but not with the issue of seniority. So the children were caught in the middle and took sides, partly because the parents were fighting with each other for their loyalty. If Marge and Bill could step back from the conflict and take a look at why each needed to be boss, they might discover the reason. Then they could slowly work out a solution.

Perhaps the first step would be to agree that no rule for the children would be made and no discipline dished out unless *both* parents agreed. They might then pick one or two issues important to the family's everyday functioning and go to work on reaching an agreement, developing rules together as a start. When everyday issues of family life are controlled by conflicting philosophies stemming from individual needs for dominance, they are very hard to solve.

So when you work out parental collaboration, it's not only a matter of recognizing the equality of the sexes, the issue we hear so much about. It also has to do with sibling behavior acquired long ago. Think about how you may have learned to behave in certain ways that affect your present family relationships, especially between you and your children, without being aware of it at all. As with Marge and Bill, if you're the oldest, you're used to seniority and probably will search for it in marriage and parenting. If you're the youngest or a middle child, you may have other expectations because of past experiences with your brothers and sisters.

Junior, the Reluctant Family Heir

Cynthia and Alan have three children: Alan, Jr. (called Junior), six, Charles, four, and Carol, two. Alan talked about how proud he was of Junior but constantly belittled him. He sided with Charlie when the children fought, even though he recognized that while Charlie cried and pleaded helplessness, he had often provoked Junior into hitting him to get his father's sympathy. Alan insisted that Junior give in to Charlie because "you're older and know more. You're more grown-up." Junior had to let Charlie play with his marbles and his models, even though Charlie didn't know how to use them and threw them all over the room. Cynthia, observing all this, couldn't understand why Alan discriminated so openly against Junior, his oldest son named after himself.

What was going on? Alan had been second in a family of three. He had an older brother and a younger sister. Alan was still bitter toward his oldest brother for bullying him when they were young. So in his mind, without being aware of it, he had "substituted" Junior, the oldest of his children, for his hated older brother and was carrying on the battle of his own childhood now that he could retaliate because he was bigger and could exercise power in his own way.

Junior was responding to the preference as if it were rational, not irrational. Naturally, as a young child, he could not understand what was going on. He could only react as if it were normal, and he began to be shaped by the role that was inflicted on him. He became increasingly withdrawn, unhappy, and shy. In school he was afraid to say what he thought and refused sports because he was afraid of being hurt.

His father's paradoxical behavior continued, and he forced Junior to play catch with him—both football and baseball. While Alan enjoyed being better than Junior (he had never been as good as his older brother at anything), he was also infuriated with Junior who played at being "stupid" and "clumsy" to get out of this uncomfortable competitive situation he hadn't asked for.

Unfortunately Alan had two images of his son. Of one he was very proud: the part of his son that resembled him and was called Junior. But in larger measure Junior resembled Alan's own oldest brother with whom he still needed to fight and try to dominate, reliving an old drama.

The family scenario could easily have taken another turn. Alan could have seen in Junior the part of himself that he was proud of, the part that had finally achieved the status of being the oldest, as he had always wanted. Then he could have enjoyed his son's success. In that case, the largest part of him would be identified with Junior rather than Charlie, the second born who really represented himself as a youngster, and he could have helped the boys progress in their relationship with each other.

Unfortunately he had not grown out of his own old relationship with his brother and was still very much involved in an unsolved struggle for power, for "becoming somebody." His sons became the victims of this.

Consider the implications of being a "Junior." It's a special role assigned at birth. Presumably you're to be the one to carry on the traditions of the "senior," to be like him, someone of whom he can be proud. It may provide a favorite position for a particular youngster in the family. It may create the opposite as well. An expectation for achievement goes with the title "Junior." Junior is supposed to be more than a chip off the old block; sometimes he's supposed to be better than the old block himself and live up to more than the father has done. "Junior" may also imply an expectation to achieve what the old block could *not* get done.

It can be a heavy burden for a child. Naming a child after oneself is a Western, particularly an American, custom. In Japan, for example, there is no such word as "Junior" because the Japanese feel it is unfair to place on a child the burden of being a replica of the father or having to compete with him.

Other, less obvious roles are cast on children too young to know or defend themselves.

The Legend of King Arthur

Father had had a younger brother who died in infancy. The whole family had mourned him for years. At times Father was even made to feel that the "wrong brother had died." He named his first son Arthur, after his dead sibling. Arthur was a bright young child but his family kept saying, "Your Uncle Arthur was going to be a very important person. It's up to you to live up to his memory." Little Arthur, constantly in the shadow of an unknown ghost, tried to imagine what he could do to please his parents. But he found the difference between what he could do and what the ideal of an "Arthur" represented to the family to be too great. So he decided to give up, did poorly in school, and was even more of a disappointment to his parents.

If Father had realized how impossible it is for one person to "be" another, particularly one who has been idealized and worshiped in the family, he would not have asked his own son to replace (and be) somebody else. He would have treated him as a new and separate individual and both would have been much happier. For the legend of Arthur was an exaggerated and unrealistic dream that could not be made real by anyone.

So, depending on your own place in your own family, you can find yourself unwittingly favoring the youngster who resembles you (or someone you loved) in your new family because of his or her position—or find yourself an old rival in one of your children. Other images of persons formerly important in one's life are all too often placed on a child and unbalance your relationship with him or her and the other children. A fair, even-handed approach toward the children is very difficult when one or more of them resembles someone from the past. The resemblance can be not only a subtle one, it can lead to a stereotyped label stamped on a child.

Don't Label Kids—They May Live Up to It

Usually we don't mean any harm when we cast our youngsters into special roles by "labeling" them; we often do it secretly to ourselves. One child may be regarded as the smart one, another the handsome or pretty child, another the natural athlete, another the musical one. These traits and talents may be real, but if we exaggerate them so that a main feature really becomes an identity for the whole child, he or she may be straitjacketed and grow into that stereotype. And there is an even darker side to labeling—if one child is seen as the troublemaker whenever there is a problem.

The Nicest Mailman in Town

The Johnsons had the nicest mailman in town. He spent so much time making friends with the children on his route that he was always several hours late. In fact everybody knew when he was sick and there was a substitute because the mail came early!

Mrs. Johnson's son Billy always ran out when the mailman came. He dashed down the steps to catch him and they would sit down on the curb talking about all sorts of things. They even traded baseball cards and sometimes played a game of ticktacktoe. Or they would toss Billy's football for a few minutes. After his friend had moved on, Billy would come in proudly with the mail, sorting it out and distributing it, just like a junior mailman.

Now Billy was six years old and in school during the week. His younger sister, Susie, took his place. She had fun going for the mail, and the mailman was just as nice to her. One Saturday Billy was playing in the yard. He heard the mailman's whistle go *tweet, tweet* as his sister ran down the steps. He looked puzzled and angry. "Hi, Mr. Mailman, let's play that little game where you carry me around on your shoulders," said Susie. "Okay, honey, I guess I've got a few minutes."

Billy was furious. After the mailman left, he socked her hard. The mail spilled all over the front steps. He was still pounding her when his mother came out. "Billy, you're always causing trouble! You're the worst bully I've ever known!" "But she has my job," he protested. "Your sister has the job this year because you're in school. Why can't you be happy like she is? You're always so gloomy and angry."

Mrs. Johnson's neighbor had been watching. "What do you mean Susie is always so happy?" Mother: "She's my little sunshine. She's always making us laugh." Neighbor: "I think she may be getting the idea that she's your pet, and so may Billy." Mother: "But he always starts the fights." Neighbor: "Wait a minute. I saw 'little sunshine' wave the mail at Billy and laugh at him as she came up the walk. Billy really is a nice kid when he's at our house. He's polite and helpful. I think you've got them labeled."

Mother went inside and thought about it. She realized that her neighbor had allied herself with Billy to help her see what she had been doing. If he had been becoming a bully, it was because he had been branded one and was living up to the role he was assigned. Maybe she should think of Billy and Susie in *different* ways instead of trying to make traits come true because she harbored them in her own mind. Billy reminded her so much of her first husband. They looked alike. For the first time she could face it: she was afraid Billy would turn out like him.

She got the children together. "Kids, I think I've been wrong in calling you the bully, Billy, and you little sunshine, Susie. One is a nice nickname and the other one is not so nice, but I don't think either one of them will do you much good. I've been assuming that Billy starts the fights and Susie does nothing wrong. That's not fair. Let's turn over a new leaf. I think we ought to let Billy get the mail on Saturdays and school vacations, since Susie gets it during the week when he's at school."

Mother had woken up to her problem before it was too late: before Billy actually lived up to his role as bully, and before

Billy and Susie began to narrow their images of themselves and each other (which would only intensify their rivalry). She had realized also that you can't always treat your children equally. There is just no way to split the mailman down the middle. What had been Billy's job needn't be taken over by Susie just because he was starting school. It might backfire and make him not want to go to school or not work because he was missing so much fun. So the idea of giving him weekends and school vacations and Susie the other days was her way of resolving it. It might not be equal, but it was fair. And she had stopped a pattern of fighting between the kids that actually came from *her* association of Billy with her first husband. Billy was getting all the anger she couldn't give her former mate because he was gone.

Did you ever hear why the famous American writer Mark Twain changed his name from Samuel Clemens? He did it to shed a label that was crowding him into a corner. Samuel Clemens was labeled as a boy who was always into mischief. He was often told in front of his sister and his two brothers that he was a troublesome son, a boy who brought no peace or comfort to the house. He didn't want to be that kind of person. So he ran away to become somebody else, someone they would all be proud of one day. He wanted people to say, "Do you remember Sam Clemens? Why, he used to live right here in Hannibal. We all knew him; he was a good boy."

He joined the men who worked the riverboats. There he created, out of his own experience, the mischievous characters Tom Sawyer and Huck Finn who became American heroes. He had turned his problem into an advantage! The river had made him happy for the first time in his life. He identified with it so strongly that he changed his name to become a part of it. The lingering call "Quarterless Twain! By the mark! M-a-a-rk Twain!" provided him with a way of finding himself a new family and home. Clemens fulfilled the role created for him in his family. As Twain, however, he converted it into other characters and some of the greatest of all American literature.*

But don't count on your children to find such a great solution on their own!

Sibling Position Is Important

Now let's consider each sibling position: the single or only child, the oldest, the middle, and the youngest—not just to help you think of yourself in such a position and what you may have brought to your present family because of it, but also to understand your own children better by putting yourself in their shoes.

THE ONLY CHILD

Only children are becoming more and more common as American families shrink. This by itself may lead to a continuation of the trend toward smaller and smaller families and even fewer children because only children frequently do not want children themselves. Or if they do want to break out of the role of being the only child and have a larger family, they may take longer learning to be parents because they have less experience. They have not grown up with children of differing ages and the opposite sex. And they can't understand why their kids fight. If you came from a larger family you're used to it. You expect it and it's easier to take as just a part of life.

They've not only had less chance for close contact with other children in early life, they have had to accommodate relatively early to the adult world. And they have had a special relationship with their parents which was never altered by the intrusion of another. The only child has never had the experience of feeling temporarily replaced, a painful but im-

*Joseph Mersand, *Great American Short Biographies*. (New York: Dell Publishing Company, Inc., 1966).

portant feeling in bringing us down to earth and making us realize we have to share the world with others.

The Little Princess

Greg and Grace were both only children. They weren't able to conceive. They badly wanted a child, so they adopted Donna when she was six weeks old. She was a beautiful child, the apple of their eye. Nothing was too good for her. When Donna was two and a half, the adoption agency suggested that a brother or sister would be good for her; another baby was available.

Greg and Grace were quite uncomfortable about the idea of a newcomer to the family and wondered if Donna would be jealous. They decided to include her in the decision and asked her if she would like a baby brother or sister. "No!" cried Donna. Greg told the agency social worker that they had made up their minds to keep the family as it was.

Donna, having personally determined this major condition of her life (that she'd not have to share her parents with anyone else), grew up to be a "spoiled" child who insisted on getting her way in much less important ways. She stayed overly attached to her parents. If they tried to go out and leave her with a baby-sitter she had severe tantrums. When it was time for school to begin, she refused to go.

Greg and Grace really didn't want another child themselves. So it was partly their wishes that Donna was reflecting when she said "No!" Many only children *want* a brother or sister for companionship. They often say they want a friend. Whether they want a sibling or not, children Donna's age are too young to decide such matters. Grace and Greg didn't have the heart to see her hurt by having to share her world with another child, since they had once been in her shoes themselves.

If they had been able to see the disadvantages of Donna's central, almost all-powerful position in the family, they could have made up for it. They could have insisted on an early preschool experience so she could learn how to play with other children. Nursery school can be very valuable for only children as early as the age of two or two and a half. They could make sure she spent plenty of overnights with friends, at her house and theirs. And longer visits, too, for instance on weekends. While the only child enjoys a favorite position in the family, he or she is in need of contact with other children and often knows it. They often create "imaginary" companions or playmates who endure much longer than those of other children who have brothers and sisters.

The only child is slightly at risk for problems and should be given special help to compensate, to learn how to get along with other children in the same age group. Only children grow into adulthood proud and exclusive owners of a set of parents. Not accustomed to other children in the home, they may initially have more difficulty joining peer groups outside. The adjustment is painful but necessary. If problems continue it's because they may have come to expect the whole world to see them as the center of attention, as their parents did. They may run back to parents when defeated or not "first" in school. This tendency toward self-centeredness can be overcome if parents are aware of the risks. Because *they* are part of it. Their whole sense of being a good parent is based on only one. So they are likely to be much more sensitive and worry more about every little thing that goes wrong. Don't magnify a cold into pneumonia! Only children *can* grow up to be happy, emotionally healthy individuals.

THE FIRSTBORN

Did you know that Karl Marx, Martin Luther King, Jr., Albert Einstein, George Washington, Harry Truman, Julius Caesar, Winston Churchill, Alexander the Great, George Patton, U. S. Grant, Theodore Roosevelt, Lyondon B. Johnson, Jimmy Carter, Benito Mussolini, and Adolf Hitler were all firstborn children? What does it mean? Perhaps nothing. But one study comparing famous firstborn and later-born historical figures concluded that because the firstborn has a life-long special access to parents by virtue of being the oldest, it gives him (or her) a certain self-righteousness and rigidity about beliefs and principles. The study asserts that firstborn males therefore make more dangerous political leaders; they're more likely to "fight than switch": of the United States presidents, eight who were firstborn have led the country into war but only one of the later-born sons did so.*

Jimmy Carter is one of the exceptions. But he was a typical bossy oldest brother, according to Gloria Carter Spann, his younger sister. She described how he would pay her a nickel for doing *his* job—picking *his* peanuts, then talk her into planting the coin in a flowerbed, promising her that a "money tree" would grow there. Later, he dug up the nickel for himself.†
He pulled this trick on his little sister repeatedly but she claims she didn't realize it for a long time. Of course, Jimmy outgrew this way of dealing with his sister and learned new ones as he succeeded in the peanut business and became president. Indeed, he seems to have turned his image from the one Gloria remembered into one characterized by honesty and this probably won the presidency for him in 1976!

Robert's Rules of Order

Robert was the oldest of four children. He was twelve and had two younger sisters and a younger brother. Robert had always been a bright child. He got A's in school, was pleasant to have around, and made his par-

---

* Irving David Harris, *The Promised Seed: A Comparative Study of Eminent First and Later Sons* (Glencoe, Ill.: Free Press, 1964).
† Lloyd DeMause and Henry Ebel (eds.), *Jimmy Carter and American Fantasy* (New York: Two Continents Publishing Group Ltd., 1977).

ents happy with his achievements and his way of knowing what they wanted done. He took considerable responsibility for the younger children, helped to train and discipline them, and was a big help in bringing them up. He was therefore given a good deal of authority. He organized the other kids to do the dishes and take out the trash. When the parents weren't home, he was in charge. The baby-sitter often deferred to him. When Robert was nine, he told his parents they didn't need baby-sitters anymore; he could do the job.

Little did his parents know what really went on! He had his own set of regulations for the other children. He often bullied them. He made them run errands and do favors for him, using his superior strength and ability to think quickly to keep them in line. His parents had given him the responsibility for the house when they were out. Robert had trouble limiting it to those times. Soon it became apparent that he not only organized the children so the family functioned smoothly, he also dominated them for his own sake.

The level of authority he assumed was really dictatorial. "Take the dog out for a walk!" "Go to the store and get me a comic book or you'll get three bruises on the arm!" Robert even developed his own little protection organization. He exacted ten cents of every child's allowance each week—then they would only get beaten up when they "deserved it." Robert had taken on more than a parental role, making rules without explaining why, administering them harshly rather than with warmth because he did not have the maturity of a parent. He had the jealousy and rivalry of a sibling plus the authority of being the oldest.

Fortunately his parents discovered their mistake. They began to remove the parental authority and helped him back into the role of a sibling. When Mother heard one of the girls crying in the kitchen and found Robert twist-

ing her arm because "she was baking cookies and probably won't eat a thing at dinner," she put her foot down:
"Robert, you're not your sister's parent! If she's eating
between meals, I'll take care of it. It's not your responsibility." Robert protested, "But what about when Scott
is doing something dangerous like riding his skateboard
in the street?" Mother answered, "Then you need to tell
me so I can stop him. It's not your job to stop him!"

Researchers have discovered that a "pecking order," if accepted, minimizes conflict.* A Norwegian psychologist discovered this in flocks of chickens. The senior hen dominates
all the others; she pecks all the other hens in the flock without
being pecked back. The next hen beneath her in rank pecks
all except the top hen. The third hen pecks all below her but
not the two top hens. The poor hen at the bottom is pecked
by all those above her and has no other hen to peck. This form
of social order reduces fighting and makes the flock more
peaceful because every hen knows where she and the others
stand. But it's rigid as well as cruel, prevents new arrangements, friendships, and associations. It's not for children.
They're not chickens.

Robert's parents had done what many parents do for the
oldest, the child they know best. They put him in charge. If
parents do this, they should only do it for brief, well-defined
periods and not allow the oldest to become a permanent "third
parent." The tendency to give power to the oldest, to have
greater expectations and share a greater amount of authority,
seems to be the modern version of the "birthright."† (In
previous centuries the oldest was openly favored and was heir
to all the parents' property.)

The oldest or first child tends to be dominant in many
families because he or she is larger and "smarter" just because of

---

* John Scott, *Animal Behavior* (New York: Dover, 1963).
† Brian Sutton-Smith and B. G. Rosenberg, *The Sibling* (New York: Holt,
Rinehart and Winston, Inc., 1970).

being ahead in age. Older siblings often use their status and physical strength to get younger siblings to do what they want. Fortunately in this case Robert's parents recognized that this had gone beyond appropriate limits, and the younger children were suffering. He had bitten off more than he could chew. Robert's parents realized they had been fooled by his adultlike behavior in front of them, flattered by the fact that he imitated them as models while setting up his own system behind the scenes. They produced corrective action, changing the boundaries and limits of authority until they were more balanced again. They clarified his role vis-à-vis their own. Robert needed to learn to be a child again.

The lesson was clear: the authority of the firstborn in the family must be closely monitored. Parents too easily give away power for the sake of convenience—power which is often used improperly.

It's natural to give the oldest more responsibility. But do recognize the limits. Another thing: it isn't necessarily fun to be responsible for younger brothers and sisters. All work and no play makes anyone dull. It interferes with one's own life. The great Western hero John Wayne recalled that the first and last time he ever used a gun in real life in the cause of justice was because of his little brother Bob. The biggest trial of Duke's life was shepherding Bob around—wherever he went. When Wayne had to take Bob along to a birthday party next door, it was the last straw. One of Duke's friends said to him, "Get that little jerk outta here." Fighting his friend then became a matter of honor—and Duke was sent home. The day was ruined. He got out his BB gun, climbed on the garage roof and shot out every balloon that had been strung in the backyard for that birthday next door.*

Probably too many expectations are placed on the firstborn because he or she is so important to the parents during a critical period in the family's development—before the next baby

* Mike Tomkies, *Duke: The Story of John Wayne* (Chicago: Henry Regnery Co., 1971).

is born. They haven't yet been able to distribute their hopes and expectations because other children haven't arrived. They are still focused on the firstborn. Firstborns are often achievement oriented and perform better in school. And they often do better in life than their brothers and sisters. The pages of *Who's Who* are dominated by firstborns (and only children). The same is true for successful executives. One obvious factor in this success rate may be the result of parents spending more time with the firstborn than later-born. They have time exclusively with each other. But it doesn't last forever; the combination of being the only child for a time and then adjusting to another is probably a very healthy one.

The Happy Times Preschool

The nursery school class was buzzing. All the children were working on puzzles. It was Parents' Day and the mothers and fathers were invited to watch, participate, and have coffee. The class had twenty children—four- and five-year-olds. Blaine's mother couldn't resist "helping him" with his puzzle. "Come on, try the middle part. The sides are easy to get. Here, I'll help." Karen's mother was hugging her for finishing her puzzle. But she had also helped Karen and done much of it for her. Now she wanted her to do another.

The teacher remembered that Blaine and Karen were both firstborn. It seemed to her that the mothers of later-born youngsters were more relaxed, let their children proceed at their own pace, and didn't always set standards for them. These kids seemed happier and were having more fun. She realized that mothers of firstborns have had less experience and so are usually more concerned about their children doing well. But she'd discuss this with Blaine's and Karen's mothers at individual conferences. She had seen how parents can step back and let a child develop more naturally when they're aware of their overinvolvement and have help from an experienced teacher in dealing with it and letting their children decide and do things for themselves.

This example is based on studies in which mothers of firstborn children were actually observed.* The studies suggested that excessive involvement of the mothers creates standards that the children must fulfill because they don't set their own goals; rather they achieve the ones set for them. While the parents give help, they are also critically expectant of higher and higher levels of performance.† So birth order creates an advantage for the oldest child. But you pay a price for it.

THE MIDDLE CHILD

The middle child also has an advantage. Not only do parents have more experience when the second one comes along; they also have expended much of their achievement expectations on the firstborn and therefore put less pressure on the next children. Middle children are freer to grow at their own pace and move where their own interests and talents lead them.

They may also suffer from "benign neglect." They may have more trouble finding themselves. They may resent their "hand-me-down" role in the family. They sometimes blend blandly into the woodwork. People have more trouble describing their personalities than they do with the oldest or youngest, who get more attention.

Betty Ford in *The Times of My Life* described the typical middle child syndrome in their son Jack beautifully: "Years ago Jack said, 'Well, I'm not the golden boy. Mike is, so don't expect too much of me.' You're always more relaxed with the second child. But Jack seemed to feel every other child was

* Irma Hilton, "Differences in the behavior of mothers toward first and later born children," *Journal of Personality and Social Psychology* 7 (1967): 282–290.
† Sutton-Smith and Rosenberg, *The Sibling*.

more special to us than he was. Mike was the oldest, so he was special. Susan was the only girl, so she was special. Steven could charm the stars out of the sky, so he was special. And poor Jack was filled with resentments." But Grandma Ford had some wise words for Betty: "Sometimes you end up loving the most difficult child more than the others; you spend so much more time trying to help work out their problems, you're so much more involved with them."

I'm Always Chasing Rainbows

Sally was the middle of three girls. She had always been close to her oldest sister, Peggy, whom she adored and followed around. She and her older sister had been good friends but now Sally was teasing Peggy almost constantly. When Peggy talked to her friend on the telephone, Sally wandered in, sat down on the couch, and pretended to read. Throughout Peggy's conversation, Sally mimicked her: "Hi, how are you?" . . . "Hi, how are you?" . . . "What did you do today?" . . . "What did you do today?" . . . "Wait a minute, my sister's bugging me." "Cut that out!" . . . "Cut that out!" . . . "Stop repeating me!" . . . "Stop repeating me!"

Peggy complained to mother, "Sally won't let me alone! She comes in my room and uses my things without asking, and she seems jealous all the time." Mother to Sally: "What's the matter, sweetie? Something's bothering you. You and Peggy used to be such good friends." Sally in tears: "She used to be my *best* friend and now she's got her own friends. She left me! I'm all alone! And you like her best because she's the smartest and oldest, and you like Patty 'cause she's the littlest and cutest. Nobody likes me!"

Luckily, Mother was able to get to the heart of the matter quickly, going beyond the teasing and harassing and finding the sadness and loneliness in Sally, the feeling of the middle child that there is nothing special about her. Middle kids often feel that being youngest or oldest is special, that their own life is hopeless because you can never change being in the middle. Paying special attention to Sally meant finding out that she had wanted guitar lessons for a long time and helping arrange them with her. Sally began to feel more secure about herself as a person. She became popular with kids in her grade as she learned guitar. And she began to realize she didn't need Peggy so desperately after all.

Some researchers* have found the middle child is most often expected to help around the house. He or she is also praised less often, even when the children are playing well together. It's just expected of the middle one. They also seem to get less time with parents for games and fun. Sometimes the relaxation of pressure allows middle children to deal more easily and comfortably with other playmates. Understandably, the middle child often becomes the mediator in the family—able to see problems between others and to help solve them.

THE YOUNGEST CHILD

The stereotype of the youngest is that of the baby. In fact, in families of three and four children the youngest is often called "baby." It's not easy being born into a world where everybody else can use a spoon or ride a bike or tie shoelaces. So you learn to get others to do things for you. The youngest may receive less discipline and is not expected to help very much with household tasks.† Rose Kennedy remembers her youngest, Ted, most fondly, as the one with the "sunny disposition" in the family.‡ (In two-child families, however, the youngest are not so sharply differentiated. They are treated more like "one of two children," and sometimes parents are even more strict with them.)

---

* Robert Sears, Eleanor Maccoby, and Harry Levin, *Patterns of Child Rearing* (New York: Harper and Row, 1957).
† Sears, Maccoby, and Levin, *Patterns of Child Rearing.*
‡ Kennedy, *Times to Remember.*

However, the old wives' tale is true—sometimes there is a tendency to overprotect the youngest and keep him or her a baby because a parent wants to hold on to *one* child to keep parenting days from being over for good. In any case, there is a tendency for the other children in the family to look upon the youngest as favored and babied. Indeed, they often participate in this "role assignment" themselves. And then make the "baby" pay for it.

Here, Stupid, Let Me Do It

Jimmy, five, was screaming. His older sisters, Claire, ten, and Francie, eight, were shouting "Hold still!" when Mother came into the kitchen. Francie was holding him down while Claire was jamming his jacket on him. Mother said, "What's going on here?" Claire (aside to Jimmy): "Look what you got us into—we'll get you later! Mommy, you told us to all get ready to go to the shopping center and he can't get ready by himself. And he won't let us do it for him. He's just a big baby."

Mother: "Wait a minute, Claire. Does he have two hands?" Claire (sulking): "Yes." Mother: "Francie, does he have two arms attached to those hands?" Francie: "Of course he does. Don't be silly, Mother." Mother: "Well, then, why can't you let him use them? It's as if everybody around here *wants* him to be the baby, *wants* to do things for him, and is mad when he won't let you. Why do we have to have a baby in the family forever? Now, Jimmy, let's see if you can get up and put on your own jacket and maybe even zip it up. We'll give you some help if you ask for it but not until you do."

You see that the youngest does have a special problem to overcome and is often assigned the role of "baby" among the other siblings. This usually means he or she is supposed to be helpless, stupid, clumsy, or playful and friendly like a doll, but is not to grow up because the family needs a permanent baby.

There is a kind of envy in this sibling rivalry. But here Mother breaks up the role assigned to Jimmy, which he fights but nevertheless fits himself into. She takes the side of his growing up, not being more helpless than he really is, and she effectively begins to break up a root cause of fighting in her family.

For the youngest, parents and siblings alike most often "mind read": "you're cold; put on a sweater" or "you're hungry; have something to eat" as if their own feelings belonged to the child, who should reflect and conform to them. But this prevents a person from growing up as an individual, from knowing who he/she is. How can you know what your own sensations and feelings are if they are always mixed up with others' who confuse them with theirs?

A few years ago conventional wisdom held that children whose speech was delayed had parents who did everything for them. They didn't need to talk to get what they wanted. Language acquisition is more complicated. It is a matter of maturation of the equipment needed to speak—the brain and its connections to the vocal cords—and the experience and practice that develops the function. Many speech problems are now known to be caused by a kind of short circuit in the way messages are received, processed, and sent out by the brain. But many cases of delayed language are reinforced by other people meeting all the child's needs without his needing to put in the work to develop speech himself. And there are even greater implications for personality development. A personal sense of helplessness is inevitable when others anticipate your every thought, need, wish, and mood. And this may last a lifetime unless caught and corrected before long.

When to Have the Second Child

We have already discussed the spacing of children and how it can affect sibling rivalry. But keep in mind that whenever a second child arrives, it's *bound* to affect whatever phase of development the first child is going through. This can't be helped. The first child will adjust. But there are more critical phases than others. Some produce more problems if interrupted than others. For example, after the first six months of life, when your baby has become almost one person with you again, almost as it was in the womb, a gradual period of separation begins.* Exploring the world by using Mother's body as one's entire world continues until about ten months. Between approximately ten and fifteen months there is a kind of practicing characterized by moving away from Mother and, finally, walking.

The next year or so is the "toddler stage" with even greater awareness of physical separateness from the mother. The child goes away and comes back when he/she finds that the world is *not* his/her oyster. He/she is constantly experimenting and gradually widening the circle of a familar outside world beyond Mother's skirts. After that, in the third year, there is a new kind of growth—the ability to function more and more smoothly alone. The three-year-old *knows* that Mother and Father are okay without having to be with them all the time.

So if you plan a second child, consider that the ten- to fifteen-month "practicing" phase is best not interrupted, if you can help it, either by starting work during that time or by a newcomer arriving in the family who takes so much of a mother's time and attention. If feasible, try to space children at least two years apart so the second year of life is not interrupted.

The ideal spacing is probably two and a half to three and a half years. Longer intervals produce different generations of children who have less to do with each other. This is why shorter intervals, one to two years, produce more intense rivalry between children. The oldest has had a major life disruption caused by the new baby that's hard to forget. The toddler period of the second year is the most vulnerable time.

* Margaret Mahler, "Symbiosis and individuation: the psychological birth of the human infant," *Psychoanalytic Study of the Child* 29 (1974): 89–106.

He/she is more and more able to adjust to a new baby as time passes. There is just no ideal time. But three is about right.

Sudden changes are hard to adjust to, especially if you're highly vulnerable and just beginning to move out on your own. But after all, we all have to live with stress. It can be dealt with, and it's an important part of learning about life, as long as you're supportive and understanding. We can't (nor should we) protect our children from *all* stress. If we wanted to avoid it completely, our children would never visit the dentist! They would certainly be protected, but overprotecting keeps them from learning to deal with things on their own. Just make sure it's in the right dose and not overwhelming.

Preparing for the New Baby

These days the typical couple wants two planned children. Be prepared for more rivalry between two than among three or more. But you can deal with it. Preventing exaggerated jealousy and minimizing normal jealousy is your goal. So begin early.

You may be surprised to know that the intensity of rivalry during the first few years is determined to a large extent around the time of birth of the second-born. So the birth of your second child is a critical point for prevention of later problems, of rivalry that is prolonged or even never outgrown. Good preparation of the firstborn is the best insurance policy you can buy. So spend the time and effort. A milligram of prevention is worth at least a kilogram of cure.

Let the Stork Take Her Back to the Store

Todd was almost two years old, his parents' first child. His mother was excited about her second pregnancy but felt Todd was too young to notice or be told about it. Just before her due date she did tell him that a wonderful new baby would be coming to their family. "We're getting her at the baby store." She even took Todd over to her neighbor's and showed him their new baby. "It will be just like that one, Todd." Father, on the other hand, told Todd the stork delivered babies. That was what he had been told as a boy.

When Mother suddenly went to the hospital, Todd was left with a new baby-sitter. He was impossible to manage and cried for his Mommy. "Why did she go away?" he wailed.

When his Mommy came home, he was mad and hit her for leaving him alone. Finding a new crib in his room, he looked at the occupant and saw no resemblance to the baby down the street. This one was cross-eyed, bald, badly wrinkled, and screaming bloody murder. Todd pinched and squeezed it to make it stop crying.

In a few days, Todd had stopped playing with his toys, clung to his mother for affection and attention, and demanded to sleep with her. Mother said, "I think he needs something all his own—something he can love and that will love him back. I know how he feels." They bought him a new puppy. Soon they had to get rid of it because Todd was obsessed with pulling its tail. If he pulled at one end, a noise came out the other! Todd and his baby sister were mortal enemies for several years, and the best they could accomplish in later life was an armed truce.

Margaret Mead, who loved children, would understand Todd. She recalls the birth of her younger brother in *Blackberry Winter*:

"Before Dick was born, my parents made the common mistake of promising me a playmate in the new baby. As a result, I found his newborn ineptitude very exasperating. I have been told that I once got him, as a toddler, behind a door and furiously demanded, 'Can't you say anything but 'da da da' all the time?' "

Jealousy of a new baby is perfectly normal. Parental attention becomes divided. If a youngster, particularly a firstborn, is not upset to some degree with the need to share his or her parents' love with the new baby, he or she either did not ever feel loved (so now doesn't miss it) or the baby is being short-changed in his/her favor.

Todd's parents could have taken several steps to reduce his mounting jealousy and anger. Young children are fearful of changes and surprises, particularly sudden ones; it's best to prepare them gradually. A two-year-old isn't too young to notice Mother's pregnancy and it can be discussed at a level he/she can understand. Two- and three-year-olds are most familiar with the digestive system. It's all they know from their own experience; they've never heard of something as fancy as the reproductive system. So they will assume that anything in the "belly" has been swallowed and will come out through the rectum. Still, you can try:

"There's another part of the 'stomach,' Todd, a special place where babies stay until they're ready to come out. Here, I'll draw it for you."

Mother's pregnancy is a natural time for early sex education. A few weeks of preparation could have softened the blow. Instead, Todd's parents told him confusing stories about where babies come from and showed him a baby down the street to make him think it could be duplicated! No wonder Todd was disappointed when his own new sister didn't look like the one he was promised.

On top of finding that he had to share his mother with the new baby, the newcomer was moved into his room, and he certainly wasn't ready to share *that*. How could he be expected to accept sharing his room when he hadn't even been told about it? It would've been far wiser (if his room *had* to be shared) to move the new crib in ahead of time. Todd could even have been invited to help pick it out so the baby would seem partly "his," not just "theirs." The last-minute peace offering (a pet to comfort him) was well-meaning but failed because it was too late. Todd was totally unprepared for the new baby and for the abrupt change in his relationship to his mother. A dog isn't interchangeable with a mother. But it could be made to squeal, as if it were the new baby!

The second year of life is probably the hardest time for a child to accept a new baby. Actress Olivia de Havilland was one year and three months older than her sister, Joan Fontaine. In her autobiography, Joan Fontaine says that Olivia was too young to share their mother with a new arrival and that she, Joan, was an "inexcusable intrusion," "an enemy." She concludes that it lasted and lasted—Joan remembers nothing pleasant between Olivia and herself all through their childhood.

The one- to two-year interval between children can be handled if it's done openly, honestly, and gradually. Remember, though, it's the time when a child is beginning to separate from Mother and be on his/her own—walking, talking, exploring beyond her skirttails (or panttails), and trying independence on for size. It's a vulnerable period, and the child is much like the lobster, shed of the old shell which was too tight and waiting now for the new one to grow over a soft body that's highly vulnerable to dangers around it.

Todd needed protection like the lobster. Mother might have driven him by the hospital to show him where she would be for a few days; she might have taken him along for one of her prenatal checkups at the doctor's office. If a familiar babysitter or a relative (like Grandmother) had moved in and made sure he had a few brief telephone conversations with Mother while she was in the hospital, he might have tolerated her absence better. The big event might have gone smoother for everyone.

A new pet *can* help. But having heard about storks from his father and the baby store from his mother, Todd was confused, uncertain, and understandably suspicious of whatever hap-

pened next. Too many surprises had hit him too fast. It was
the first time his mother had been away for longer than a day
and no one whom he knew was around to comfort him. He
was mad at Mother for leaving him and mad at the baby for
coming into the house. ("I want the baby to go away!")

While it's true that one- or two-year-old children are generally not as openly inquisitive about a new baby as older
ones, it's even more important for parents to be sensitive to
their needs and to prepare them. At their age it's easy to become "allergic" to the new baby, just as they become allergic
to milk and eggs. They are more than lobsters. During these
early years, the immaturity of their psychological *as well* as
their biological system makes them doubly vulnerable.

Okay, If That's What They Want, I'll Give It to 'Em

Ellen, three and a half, noticed her mother's enlarged
abdomen at the fifth month. Ellen had been an only
child, and Father had shared much of her care with
Mother since birth. He took turns staying with her, feeding, and changing her. They had fun playing together.

Mother and Father explained the pregnancy to her and
showed her a picture book describing how new babies are
born. Mother put Ellen's hand on her belly so she could
feel the baby move and realize it was actually there. They
lived in a one-bedroom apartment and were planning to
move to a larger one. But Father said, "Let's not move
around the time the new baby is coming. I think Ellen
will be more frightened by a new and strange place than
by our cramped quarters here. This place is familiar to
her. And she likes her room so much."

Mother told her that the baby would have to sleep in
a crib in their room. "Ellen, you'll probably be mad and
jealous about that for a little while. But don't worry.
You'll get over it." They bought a crib, put it in their
room, and let Ellen try it out herself from time to time.

She liked it. Ellen happened to be due for a new bed of her own soon. So they let her pick out a four-poster, just like Mom and Dad slept in, and she felt grown-up.

When Mother went to the hospital, Ellen was able to visit almost any time because of the new, more flexible rules. When Mother came home with Bert, the new baby, Ellen got a new doll as a present. She didn't care for it that much. She watched all her aunts, uncles, and cousins who came over and crowded around Bert's crib. "Oh, what a cute little thing" and "You're a little punkin" was all Ellen heard from the people who used to think that *she* was so cute.

She felt left out. After a few days of this, she began to wonder what was so great about a baby who couldn't do anything but make noise and squirt from both ends.

Okay, Ellen thought to herself, *if that's what they want that's what I'll do too. All this business about acting grown up sure doesn't get you anywhere!*

Ellen began to wet her bed occasionally and had a tantrum when she didn't get her way. But her parents were patient and understanding, and Father made a point of stepping in and spending more time with her in the evenings, playing games, putting her on his lap to read stories, and giving plenty of hugs.

In this case, Father, who had been involved in child rearing throughout Ellen's life, was able to step in easily and take a larger role so that the temporary loss of Mother to Bert was not so jarring an event for Ellen.

One day Mother was surprised when Ellen said, "I guess you're not my Mommy anymore." And Mother began to realize that to a three-year-old mind it's a matter of one to one: one mother to one child. Now she was able to explain away this fear that had been gnawing at Ellen inside, and she arranged for swimming lessons once a week, just for Ellen and herself.

Some cultures have a custom to help with the arrival of a new baby.* A member of the clan—uncle, aunt, or cousin— "adopts" the next child and gives him/her special attention and care. It's almost as if the child who is displaced by the new baby becomes a new baby him/herself. Perhaps our culture, with so many families choosing godparents for a child at birth, should postpone this event and make it mean more—when the child is two or three and really needs one.

In any case, Ellen's parents had prepared her well enough for the new baby and the process around it. They had done it *slowly* over a long enough time.

It's a good idea for parents to begin to talk to their young-sters about the new baby during the second trimester, when the pregnancy is visible and quickening occurs—the baby moves. It might be wise to discuss it even earlier if Mother has morning sickness and periods of the blues. Youngsters need to understand these changes in mood and not think that they did something that's causing Mommy not to feel well.

The idea is: children should have enough (and the right kind of) information to make for the smoothest transition possible. Try to avoid telling too much to small children or too little to older ones.

Ellen's parents decided that familiar surroundings were re-assuring to her and that two big events—a move to a new apartment and the arrival of a baby—would be harder for Ellen to handle than adjusting to the baby sleeping in their room for a while. Of course it's better for the baby to have a room of its own but that isn't always possible. Ellen's loss of center stage in the family and her temporary letting go of hard won accomplishments (such as toilet training and self-control) are quite normal. Fortunately her parents took it in stride and were able to give her the support she needed so that she soon resumed growing up instead of growing back-ward.

* Jane Briggs, *Never in Anger* (Cambridge, Mass.: Harvard University Press, 1970).

Studies have shown that the stronger the bond is between the older child and the mother, the greater the disturbance a new baby will cause to it, and the greater the overt rivalry and hostility. The older the child (and the less exclusive the bond, i.e., someone else, like Father, has shared early child rearing), the less likely its emotional life is so wholly tied up with the mother.*

In a larger family, it's much more likely that the youngest child has close attachments to older siblings that buffer the reaction to a new baby. The youngsters often help educate each other about the coming of a new baby. In Ellen's case, her father had played a major role in her care; he acted in place of an older brother or sister, as well as for himself and his wife.

Rockabye, Baby

Lisa, seven, and her brother Mark, three, were well prepared for the new baby. Lisa was able to understand a good deal about how babies were born and explained things to Mark when he asked her about it. Lisa was wondering whether it would be a boy or a girl. She wanted a sister. Mark was more concerned with Mommy being away for a couple of days at the hospital. He went back to sucking his thumb. The new crib was put in Lisa's room because she wanted it there. She saw the new baby as a chance to have a "new friend." She had seen Zsa Zsa, their German shepherd, give birth to puppies and wanted to see the baby come. But that wasn't possible. When Mother went to the hospital Daddy went too because they had chosen Lamaze delivery, and Grandmother stayed with the youngsters.

When Mother came home, Lisa wanted to hold the baby. She felt a little annoyed when Mother was feeding the baby and sometimes even sneaked the new pacifier

* David Levy, *Studies in Sibling Rivalry*, American Orthopsychiatric Association, Research Monograph, no. 2, edited by Lawson Lowrey (New York, 1937).

into her own mouth for a good suck or two. But she was glad the baby was a girl and had helped pick out her new name, Betsy. She also began spending time with Mother in the kitchen and felt quite grown-up when she helped with the cooking. Mark, on the other hand, was having lots of trouble sleeping and wouldn't go to bed.

He said, "I'm afraid Mommy is going to die." Father: "Why, Mark?" Mark: "Because her hair is getting gray."

His father got exasperated with him because the night-time feedings already caused him some loss of sleep. Mark's constant dawdling, asking for glasses of water, and crying out to see where his parents were after the lights were out was getting to Daddy. He felt Mark was just manipulating. "That's the last time, Mark. One more time and I'll have to lock the door to your room."

But Lisa took an interest in Mark's problem and said, "Daddy, don't be so mad at Mark. He's having bad dreams about lions and tigers eating him up. If you went to bed one night and found a lion or tiger there, would you want to go back?"

Father began to understand. He got a night-light for Mark and read him one extra story at bedtime. Mark's old security blanket was dug out of the closet and he welcomed it back as an old friend, temporary protection against the wild animals. He forgot about it after a few weeks and slept just fine.

Because Lisa was older and had already experienced the negative feelings that come home with a new child, she found it much easier to adjust to her new baby sister. She wanted to be part of the parenting process herself. Helping Mother with the baby and helping Father with Mark even brought a *spurt* in her development. This is often a dividend from the birth of a new sibling, especially if a youngster can feel proud of being more grown-up and finds this appreciated by the parents. Lisa had also seen the process of birth when the puppies were born and was old enough to be able to understand it. She could take care of her pangs of jealousy when she watched the baby being fed.

Lisa wanted a sibling of the same sex because this can be reassuring to some youngsters; that is, the new child is a boy or a girl just like themselves. On the other hand, they may prefer a child of the opposite sex who is seen as less competition. This may have been true with Mark, because he didn't show open regression or anger toward Mother or the baby. Instead it was indirect, the nightmares. But he also had the support of an older sister who shared his predicament and handled it well. That helped him. Nevertheless, as the youngest, he was still closer to his mother and had never had the experience of a new baby in the family to cope with.

Lisa was able to move forward with an emotional growth spurt and further independence. Mark's problems about the new baby were harder to swallow. He showed these in his nightmares of people being eaten up by ferocious animals. These scenes probably represented the deep down way he felt inside toward the baby, coupled with a guilty conscience for feeling that way.

Lyndon Johnson would have understood Mark. He told about a memory or dream he had when he was five. In it he was playing catch with his oldest sister. The younger sister was in her crib crying. He threw the ball at her, straight and fast. His mother, who was pregnant, stepped right in the path of the ball and it hit her hard right in the abdomen. Lyndon was certain her belly would pop open like a balloon.

Younger brother Sam was born anyway, in spite of Lyndon's dream. He grew up in Lyndon's shadow but was always taken care of by his older brother when he needed help.*

Lisa saw Mark's problem from a sibling's point of view, very different from that of her father. His own sleep was threatened

* Doris Kearns, *Lyndon Johnson and the American Dream* (New York: Harper and Row, 1976).

and he reacted irritably to Mark's delaying tactics at bedtime. But Lisa understood that it was more due to fear than to stubbornness. She was closer to it than Father. She had been there.

Mark's negative reactions to the new baby and his mother were softened and dealt with inwardly through nightmares and fears for his mother. For Lisa, the positive aspects of the new family situation outweighed the negative. While the baby deprived her of certain old satisfactions, it also brought new ones. It allowed her to feel more grown-up, not only by helping Mark because she "knew what it was like," but also by helping Mother take care of Betsy. When she started to help in the kitchen, her own relationship with her mother became even closer than it had been.

Lisa was assuming a new healthy role in the family and probably would become a better person for it, more secure and capable than if there had not been a baby. For Mark, good preparation and support from his parents was as important in helping him to readjust as having an older sister. There is no question: the most difficult adjustment is between two adjacent siblings. If it is handled well, they can grow out of their rivalry to become good friends. If not, they can become enemies for life and their relationship with each other may well extend to fighting with other children outside the home.

Why More Than One?

If you miss one major event in life—having to share your parents with someone else—you're not really ahead. I've mentioned why it may be a disadvantage to be an only child with a very special relationship to the parents. The normal fears and worries of parents over their firstborn may continue and become exaggerated precisely *because* he/she remains their only one. They may limit what he can do, e.g., playing outside with other children and taking the chances of life that are necessary in the real world to become independent and self-reliant.

There's no such thing as an ideal size for a family. But a child lacking brothers and sisters can be at a disadvantage. I've suggested before: sibling rivalry is a part of growing up. It's not essential. But it's important. Every human being has a range and combination of feelings toward others—love, hate, and jealousy included. For a small child, it's much easier to experiment with these emotions toward brothers and sisters than toward parents. You can only understand and come to control these feelings that make us human by experiencing them.

Jealousy toward a new sibling is normal and almost universal. You must naturally protect the newborn child so the older can't harm him or her. Do try to accept that the older can't be expected to welcome the newcomer. Show your youngsters that the new baby has not basically changed anything between you and them; they're loved just as much as before. As soon as they really feel this, that the new baby truly does not make them less wanted, they'll stop worrying. They may even begin to like the newcomer.

Often jealousy and rivalry don't surface at the time of birth when it seems most likely. The new baby is relatively helpless and harmless. When the baby becomes a toddler at a year or year and a half, he or she will begin to bother the older children, getting into their things. Then the rivalry may begin, a delayed reaction.

Having to deal with brother-sister fighting is an inevitable part of raising children. Unfortunately many of us feel that we should be tax exempt from it, that it should somehow not occur, and that it's abnormal when it does. Shouldn't family members love each other?

I think most parents are so upset by it because they didn't expect it. But look at the reverse side of the sibling coin. As we've seen, if the first child remains an only child, he or she stays the special focus of parental worries and concerns. Both the youngster and parents are released from this when a second one comes along. Just becoming a two-child family breaks parents loose from this pattern. It gives them a "second wind." The price one must pay is the fighting and jealousy between the kids. You can, believe it or not, develop a strategy and a variety of tactics based on what is best for the youngsters and guide them toward a solution of their rivalry. It will make them better for having gone through it, not worse.

Parental Malpractice—Rejection and Preferences

So far you may have the impression that jealousy between brothers and sisters decreases with more children and each child is progressively easier for parents to handle. This is not always true, especially if the circumstances around a particular child's birth made him unwanted.

Did You Ever Want to Murder Your Little Brother?

Brad, four, had bitten his sister, Susan, ten, on the arm. He was screaming in pain because she had socked him in the head. Mother came and took Brad in her arms. Michael, twelve, said, "Brad started it, Mother. He bit Susan because she wouldn't give him her cookie while they were watching TV." Father, who had been reading the paper, was disgusted with the whole thing and said, "Brad is nothing but a baby and a mama's boy—always was." Susan echoed his sentiment, "And he's a spoiled brat." Mother picked up Brad and carried him to the kitchen, saying, "But he's hungry, aren't you, my little darling?" (Brad had not been hungry; he just wanted his sister's cookie.) "Let me get you something to eat." Michael said, shaking his head, "If Mother only understood how he bugs us." Father shrugged: "What can you do?"

Father *could* have done something. He could have laid down a rule that there was to be no biting in the house, no matter what, because it was dangerous. He could have also taken firm action against Brad, who liked to hit and throw things, then run away. He constantly provoked his older brother and sister. Occasionally, Father did discipline Brad, but only with severe spankings. In general, he had washed his hands of Brad before Brad was even born. Brad was an unwanted child.

He was unplanned and arrived when his mother was menopausal. Father was having business reverses. A basically sound marriage was in a stormy period. Mother had been ill throughout the pregnancy. Brad was a fretful baby, irritated his father and worried his mother. Father's rejection of Brad was out in the open. The older children imitated it because it was the way they felt too. Mother, on the other hand, dealt with her negative feelings toward Brad by covering them up with overconcern.

If she indulged his every wish—in fact, read his mind and took care of hunger pangs before he even had to feel them— how could she possibly not want him? Besides, the tension with her husband made her turn to Brad more and more for comfort. She was secretly afraid her husband might leave her. If Brad remained a baby, how could she be growing old and unattractive? She must still be young to be a mother with a new baby, and you had to anticipate a baby's every need. It was only as they grow older that you need to let go and not "feel" for them.

Emotional rejection of one child paralyzes or twists the parents' handling of sibling rivalry. In this case, Father fed the problem by his open rejection of Brad, and Mother by her overindulgence. In many other families, both parents may reject the child and their attitudes are adopted not only by the other siblings, but by the unwanted child himself because he feels hurt and angry. How can he get back at his mother and father who are so big? It's much easier to provoke and attack brothers and sisters.

In spite of modern contraception, unplanned pregnancies still occur. Some, of course, produce children who become wanted. Others remain unwanted, particularly if they come along at a difficult time—when a new addition to the family is particularly stressful or if the pregnancy is *the* reason for marriage or keeping a marriage together. The child is a constant reminder that one or the other's freedom was given up for the baby.

Rejection of a child, primarily emotional, is often physical as well. During the past decade, child abuse has been uncovered as a major national public health problem. This is the first time we've begun to see how surprisingly many rejected and unwanted children are with us. In Brad's case, both parents had tried to accept the baby. But with Father, underlying resentment prevailed. Mother, who couldn't accept the resentment in herself, had the opposite reaction: overprotection and overindulgence.

The roadblocks to the whole family's growth, not just Brad's, will be hard to overcome unless the parents are able to openly face the problem their other children are trying to point out to them. Sometimes a determined, conscious effort can overcome underlying resentment toward a child. But the resentment must first be acknowledged, or illogical and irrational behavior toward the child will never be faced.

It's not too late to lay down some rules for Brad and help him become a civilized member of the family. Mother will also have to lay down a rule for herself: "I'm not allowed to tell Brad how he feels about everything. He's no longer in his infancy, when mothers have to guess and anticipate these things."

Comparing Children to Each Other

How about other forms of rejection such as parental preference of one child over another? More common than blatant rejection, it's no less damaging. Happily, it's easier to face and reverse.

As a boy, Winston Churchill was always being compared unfavorably with his brother Jack, who was younger by four years. Their mother wrote to the father that Winston was a bad example for Jack, a "good" child whom "naughty" Winston was urged to imitate. Winston wrote home apologizing over and over again and begging for forgiveness.* But he somehow overcame this handicap. Perhaps it was a combination of an iron constitution and sheer determination. It worked. How many of us ever knew that there even was a brother Jack?

Why Can't You Get A's Like Your Sister?

Jane, ten, and Dan, eight, were pleasant, attractive children. Dan was popular and athletic. His sister was more of a student. Mother had been a schoolteacher. She tried to get Dan to work harder in school by pointing out his sister's good grades and how much she studied for them: "Look how well Jane does, Dan. You could do that if you only tried harder."

Dan was trying as hard as he could. He got B's and C's in school, but was beginning to wonder: Was it worth trying at all? He felt especially humiliated at report card time when Jane, beaming, brought out her report card at the dinner table and showed how well she was doing. "Where's your card, Danny?" asked Mother.

---

* Randolph Churchill, *Winston S. Churchill, Volume 1. Youth* (Boston: Houghton Mifflin Co., 1966).

Not surprisingly, Dan was keeping it in his books upstairs as long as he could because it was only B's and C's. *Next time,* he thinks to himself, *I'll lose it on the way home from school.* But before next report card time he'll certainly have started more than his share of fights and arguments with Jane, who had begun to call him "stupid" when his parents couldn't hear.

Mother really felt she was helping spur Dan on by making the comparison to his sister. His grades reflected her priorities of what's important in life. Don't forget, she had been a schoolteacher. The preference she gave to Jane was bound to build up more and more resentment in Dan. He wasn't stimulated by the comparison. He felt defeated and put down.

Jane, sensing a family value system which stressed intellectual superiority, worked harder and harder to be intellectually superior. She gave up a good deal of the personal and social side of life at school in favor of what was rewarded at home. To make herself feel even more important, she rubbed it in by telling Dan, "I'm in, you're out." Then she highlighted the report card discussion by staging it at dinner in public, when the family was all together.

Mother or Father might have said: "Let's talk about report cards another time. Let's talk about what you all did at school that was most fun today." That way, Jane's exaggerated feeling of superiority would not have been reinforced. It would be better to deal with each child and his or her report card individually and privately, telling Jane that she was doing well but expressing hope that she was enjoying other things as well. The parents could assure Dan that B's and C's were fine if he was doing his best and was enjoying learning. Maybe then he would grow to like his C courses better. It would have been especially helpful to compliment him on being elected vice-president of his class and making the soccer team— very important events, too, especially for boosting his self-esteem.

Preferred and nonpreferred children soon pick up who has greatest value to the parents and why. Everyone loses when there is a preferred child. This doesn't mean you must treat every child exactly the same. Everyone is different, so it's a very good idea to relate differently to the specialness of each of your children. This can and should be done without assigning greater value to one over the other. In the last illustration, it could have worked just the opposite if Father and Mother had placed more emphasis on popularity and athletics than academics. This would have been just as bad for Jane and Dan; they would merely have suffered in different ways.

Sometimes parental preferences are intentional and openly destructive. The successful Broadway play and movie *The Lion in Winter** gives a good example. It portrays England's King Henry II and Queen Eleanor not only fighting *over* their sons but also delighting in producing envious competition in them. The sons' confusion is best expressed by Prince John, who had *thought* he was his father's favorite and reveled in it, but then learned it was only a game King Henry was playing. He cries helplessly that Geoffry was smart, and Richard (the Lionheart) was brave, but he was nothing!

Other times it happens by accident of fate or circumstance. Sophia Loren's younger sister recalls their life in postwar Rome.† Her mother and Sophia went out from morning till night for almost two years searching for acting jobs for Sophia. Maria, eleven, was left in their single room, terrified at being alone, especially when it was dark. It was clear which was more important: Sophia's career, not Maria's fears. She suffered— no question. But she could compensate, partly because Sophia didn't take unfair advantage of her special role in the family to make things worse for Maria. Instead, Sophia, who is de-

---

* James Goldman, *The Lion in Winter*. Basic Catalog of Plays (Hollywood, Ca.: Samuel French, Inc.).

† A. E. Hotchner, *Sophia: Living and Loving* (New York: William Morrow and Company, 1979).

scribed by those who know her as not only a beautiful and gifted actress, but a warm and generous person, seemed to provide the strength and support which Maria needed to survive emotionally. The destructive effects of preference were blunted.

It's hard for parents not to fall into the habit of comparing brothers and sisters. It sounds so natural: "Linda takes better care of her clothes and keeps her room neat"; "Look how well Jimmy eats." Instead of working *for* you, this comparison shopping will almost always work against you. It'll produce anger and resentment in the undervalued child, and the hostility will be beamed toward the child who is being held up as the model as well as toward the parents. It'll be directed toward himself as well. He may begin to feel crushed by the touted superiority of the sibling and this can make him lose all desire to do better.

Jane, in this case, knowing the source of her power in the family, believes that her superiority is real, that the rest of the world feels this way also. So she works harder to excel in the one activity she believes to be the key to all success and happiness. And for a very weighty reason: she has been led to believe that the world beyond her family is also organized according to *their* personal preference. A powerful motivator!

When one child is the favorite of one parent and the other child the favorite of the other, the youngsters' personality characteristics will be exaggerated to please the parent who values them. Feelings of inferiority and rivalry will focus on the traits of the other sibling, the ones favored by the other parent. For example, if Dan's father had emphasized athletic achievement and popularity as values to be most admired, Jane might very well have basked in her A's, but felt inferior and resentful because of her lack of achievement in extracurricular activities. She couldn't just accept these as Dan's very personal strengths.

Sex and Gender Preferences

The Crown Prince

Carl could do no wrong. He was a handsome child from birth. Now, at six, he acted like a ruling despot in the family. He demanded the prerogatives of royalty as his birthright. He shouted at his sisters, eight and four, to fetch things for him and give in to his very wish. He knew that he was prized as the only male descendant in his father's family and would carry on the family name because his father kept saying so: "We'll all be proud of Carl someday! He'll carry on the family name. I can't wait till he has grandchildren for us."

Carl could boss around his younger sister Lucy, but Terry, two years older, fought with him continually. She preferred to play with his toys instead of hers and loved to beat him at games. Mother also obviously preferred Carl: "What if he did eat all the cookies, Terry? You're a big girl and shouldn't mind." So Terry decided to be like him. She refused to wear girl's clothing, dressed like a boy, and said being a girl was "junk" because girls were "sissies."

Nothing is more potentially serious for distorting personality development (as well as complicating and intensifying sibling rivalry) than parents preferring one sex over the other. The child of the "wrong" gender will feel disappointed in his or her sex, whichever it is.

Terry very openly acknowledged that she recognized one had to be a boy to be important in her family. So she decided to try to be one, too. She would be doomed to failure. It's hard to become something you're not biologically able to be. Her own feelings of inferiority would become exaggerated. They'd be taken out on Carl more and more as she felt increasingly discouraged at her unsuccessful search for recognition.

If Carl's father had preferred Terry, a girl, Carl might have developed a wish to be a girl to express his envy of his sister and his competition for his father's love and attention. He might become uncomfortable with his own sex and also have problems with the opposite sex as he grew up. So it can work either way. Either way is harmful.

Parents who express a preference, directly or indirectly, for children of one sex will most likely be blind to the talents and abilities of the children of the opposite sex. (In this case, Terry had considerable musical and intellectual talents.) So these talents will rarely become fully developed. Often they are also deprecated by the youngster, who believes that the parental preference for the opposite sex is based on reality and reflects actual superiority. And the favored children overestimate and exaggerate the qualities they believe established their superiority because they want to continue it. Just being a little boy was enough for Carl because in that role he could get whatever he wanted.

In fact, Carl's role assignment reflected his father's uncertainty about himself and his own ineffectiveness as a man. He chose Carl to represent his own wishes for recognition and position in the family. His own situation was unenviable. He was unsuccessful in his job and had no outside friends. Instead, Carl was his best friend. He took Carl to the zoo and the beach on weekends, leaving the girls at home. His son could do no wrong. If only Carl and Terry were old enough to realize that the wide difference in their status in the family represented not defects in them but a problem in their father, they might not have tried so hard to conform to try to fit the picture he wanted. Unfortunately they were too young to know, only old enough to react.

To the neighbors, the father seemed irrational in his preference for his son, but to his young children, he was a knowledgeable and important person to be pleased. If the mother had been stronger, she might have tried to balance the father's view of the children, pointing out Terry's abilities and talents and expressing her own appreciation of Terry: "Come on, Terry, let's try playing the piano together." Or "Your homeroom teacher says you're one of the best students in the class."

Cross-sex preference (the mother preferring a son and the father a daughter) often leads to distortion and serious difficulties in growing up to be a young man or young woman with a healthy pride in one's maleness or femaleness.* A boy must learn to be masculine and at the same time soft and tender, and a girl to be assertive without losing her femininity.

Not long ago it was common for parents to direct their children into activities that were considered suitably "male" or "female." Fathers were often particularly concerned that their sons be good in science, math, and athletics. Mothers and fathers encouraged their daughters to be good at cooking, talented in the creative arts: dance, music, and drawing. Often if a youngster wasn't physically well coordinated or didn't have a good capacity for imagery, it was like trying to force a born left-hander to become right-handed. Now there is less association of skills with maleness and femaleness. But many families still do link them with gender and new problems of parental gender preference are cropping up with the changing times.

Wonder Woman

Joan was captain of her tenth grade volleyball team and all-city. She was getting honors in science and wanted to be a doctor. George, in the eighth grade, was less outstanding, but a solid student and had his own interests and skills which he channeled into intramural team sports. He had also made the eighth grade glee club. A typical dinner table conversation with the family:

Father: "Joan, tell us about your volleyball practice this afternoon."

* Irving Bieber, "Pathogenicity of parental preference," *Journal of the American Academy of Psychoanalysis* 5(3):391–398.

Joan tells.

Mother: "And I bet you got another A in the science test yesterday."

Joan acknowledges.

Father: "It's going to be great to watch that championship volleyball match this Saturday. I've gone to every game this season."

By this time, Joan is uncomfortable, perhaps feeling a little guilty for being the center of attention and monopolizing all her parents' admiration and interest. So she is only picking at her favorite roast beef dinner.

George: "Hey, Joanie, you're pretty . . . ugly! Ha, ha. Look, Dad, she's not eating anything. How's she going to be able to play volleyball?"

Mother: "Joan, why don't you eat like your brother does? Use your knife and fork and stop picking at your food with your fingers."

It's fine for parents to be proud of their youngsters' achievements, particularly with Joan working on a new and different image. But when parents completely forget to balance their interest in one child with an interest in the other, they're asking for trouble between the two youngsters. It's especially difficult (but even more important) when one child is clearly outstanding intellectually, athletically, or socially and the other is not. In this case, Joan had a double edge on George. She was not only better at sports and science, but in the limelight because of the emphasis on girls' accomplishments.

Her parents were especially proud. She was unique. It would be wise if they deliberately made an effort to single out George's accomplishments, to watch an intramural game and attend the glee club concerts. They need to make an effort to look for what he does well and support his accomplishments as much as Joan's. Otherwise, keeping up with Joan will get more and more difficult for George as he becomes more and more bitter. All he can do now is get brownie points for being a good eater.

That's not much for an eighth grader, but at least it's something. And it does get Joan in trouble a little. She lets him have these crumbs. It's about all she can do, because she's unhappy, too.

Today's Changing Sex Roles

Boys and girls not only envy the other sex but also consider their own sex "better" than the other. Boys have probably had their feelings reinforced more by our society. This appears to have been a source of sibling rivalry in the past, that is, jealousy of the other sex. A shift is occurring. Today the sexes are considered *different* from each other, neither one better or valued more than the other. During this transition period, the pendulum swing may be more difficult for boys to adjust to than girls.

Girls Have More Fun

Betty, fifteen, and Hal, thirteen, were both taking physical education at school. One morning at breakfast, Hal was looking at the sports page. Hal: "They ought to have open tournaments. How come women want as much prize money as the men unless they are willing to play against them?" Betty, rising to the bait: "Lots of people want to see women play because they have a different style." Hal: "Oh, brother, a *different style!* Just like at school. Now we have mixed volleyball teams. But the girls don't care about the game. They're just worried about their *bodies.*" Hal squeals, imitating a girl: " 'Oh, I'm so fat!' What kind of a game can you have with dumb attitudes like that?" Betty: "Well, just remember when Billie Jean beat that guy for the Battle of the Sexes Tennis Championship of the World." Hal: "Yeah, that 'guy' must have been at least eighty-five years old. He looked awful! I hear he even plays in a wheelchair!" Betty: "Well, anyway, girls are less violent in sports. They get mad less and don't throw their rackets or cause as much trouble. You never see the women tennis players giving the finger to the fans." Hal (changing the subject): "It just isn't fair. Girls get all the breaks. Look at the new addition to the gym they're building for them at school." Betty: "That's because we didn't have anything before. Boys had all the equipment and facilities." Hal: "Well, you're sure making up for it now. You get practice suits *and* game suits, and I have to write a number on an old T-shirt with a crayon. And the girls get twenty basketballs and we get eight. What kind of equality is that?" Betty: "It's to make up for past injustice. So there!"

The parents let this one go on. There is no point in interrupting a decent argument. Note that the issues go beyond simple sibling rivalry. They relate to the changing roles of boys and girls.

That evening the issue was battled out in a different way. Father: "Look, I don't want him helping you cook dinner. He ought to be out there practicing a sport with the other guys." Mother: "Dear, just on a practical level, men are expected to cook for themselves more and more. And girls had better know how to change a tire, get a job, and physically protect themselves. Things are changing. In our day, boys were expected to be independent, assertive, competitive, logical, and self-confident. *That* was the real Boy Scout oath! And women were supposed to be eager to please, sensitive, and able to express tender feelings. And guess which personality traits were considered best? You don't need a Gallup Poll to answer that one! Boys had to cover up their emotions or they'd be called sissies. The only safe outlet was sports, and that was for emotions like aggression."

Father: "Okay, maybe that was wrong. But you know, I asked Hal what he wanted to be the other day and he said he didn't know. What kind of an answer is that?

Maybe he's confused." Mother: "I think it's because he's
wondering how wide a range of choices you'll let him have
or whether you're going to stick to the world as it was
growing up in our day. He doesn't know whether he's
free to choose to be a schoolteacher or a social worker instead of a policeman or an engineer. I have the feeling
Betty is going to be the doctor or lawyer and that he
would like to do other things."

Father: "But that might make him, you know, effemi-
nate." Mother: "I think we've got to separate gentleness,
warmth, and sensitivity to the feelings of others from
being feminine. Maybe what you're really worried about is
homosexuality. I think women as well as men are going
to have to begin accepting gentleness in our sons and preparing them for more of the tenderness and sensitivity
that's been emphasized for women in the past. Maybe we
need help to understand the difference between homosexuality and gentle humanity; I know that anything that
smacks of homosexuality is upsetting to both of us."

Father: "I guess you're right. It's probably a good idea
that she take shop and he take home economics so they
can see what it's like to be in the other's shoes. I mean,
well, I'm trying to come around. And I'm doing it slowly.
I guess maybe things are different and there will be a lot
more crossing over lines. I have a feeling it's going to make
it difficult for the boys for a while. I think Hal is right.
Girls are getting a lot of the attention and the spotlight
today and it's taken away something from the boys. Sports
used to be mostly for them. Now that's all changed.
They'll just have to find a way to get used to it." Mother:
"It's hard for both of them. In a way, I think they envy
each other less than girls and boys used to, but in a different way. Maybe we should swim with the tide and encourage him to develop the kinds of things he inherited
from us but didn't used to be encouraged in boys as much
as other things. Like his talent writing poetry. There cer-

tainly are differences between the sexes and the things they can do, but I think we created a lot of them in our minds. Those are the ones we need to get rid of."

Sex stereotyping crippled boys as well as girls in the past. When certain traits are considered purely masculine (such as strength and independence), or purely feminine (such as tenderness and emotionality), there isn't much freedom to choose from both sides and become a more complete person. Now studies have shown that people who comfortably combine male and female traits are best able to deal with life and the great variety of problems it presents. The new adjustments are tough on everybody, but because of the changes, your children will get along better with the other sex when they grow up.

III

MANAGEMENT

Will They Outgrow It?

Yes, they can outgrow it. Youngsters are constantly changing. Your job is to treat them differently as they do change.

Many mothers of teenagers say, "I never thought they'd stop fighting; I never thought they'd outgrow it. Now they're friends, if you can imagine!" These mothers were doing right. They were learning to help their children move along, dealing with them in changing ways as they grew up. Perhaps they didn't know it, but they were not asking too much too soon or too little too late. They had hit on just the right amount.

The key is to understand your children's development as a flow, a process that moves, as all growth, toward higher levels of functioning. If you *flow* with the process that's happening inside them, you'll more likely find success. Imagine you're a strong swimmer and suddenly encounter a crosscurrent with forces fighting each other that are stronger than you. Your best bet is to *flow* with the current, not fight it. Otherwise, you'll only exhaust yourself and maybe drown.

I've been zeroing in on the many issues of rivalry—and what to do and not do—mostly as if they're disconnected events. Now let me talk about them as a connected process, a chain that continues throughout childhood. Let's move through differing levels of conflict between children and ways to deal with them that shift so they'll reflect their new levels of personality functioning. A psychologist named Lawrence Kohlberg has

described stages of *moral* development children pass through.*
Let's try to apply this idea to sibling rivalry.

Traveling with your children through childhood and helping
them work out better ways of dealing with each other is like
traveling in a foreign country. You can't expect people there to
speak English just because you do. You're in their territory.
You need to learn to get along, to understand them, and to
learn at least a few phrases they'll understand. There's no point
in speaking English to someone who only speaks and understands Spanish.

Remarkably that's often the way parents talk to children
about their fighting. They use a different language and expect
to be understood.

To carry the analogy further, if you want to take a summer
vacation and drive from Western to Eastern Europe you'll
have to go through several countries. Most likely you will try
to pick up a few phrases in the language of each country you
pass through. At least you won't insist on everyone using English everywhere you go, or even the language from the neigh-
boring country as you move to the next one. If you learn a little
French when in France and next travel through Germany,
you'll try to shift gears. You'll listen and try to understand
some German, read the signs, and perhaps pick up a few
phrases of your own. At least you won't keep speaking French
to someone new who only speaks and understands German.
You'll keep learning to adjust as you move along through different countries.

The same should hold true for learning the language of the
"countries" our children pass through during their growing up
years.

* Lawrence Kohlberg, "Early education: a cognitive-developmental approach,"
Child Development (December 1968): 1013–1062.
Lawrence Kohlberg, "Moral education in the school," *School Review* 74
(1966): 1–30.
Lawrence Kohlberg and Carol Gilligan, "The adolescent as a philosopher: the
discovery of the self in a postconventional world," *Daedalus* 100 (1971):
1051–1086.

Let's take a family of four: Mother and Father and two children, Steven and Joy, and follow them through childhood. First, consider a couple of examples that illustrate what I mean by the "language problem"; then watch the shifting need for using a new "language" at each stage of development I'll describe and how Steven and Joy "outgrow" their rivalry with parental help.

How Things Go Wrong

To Market, To Market . . .

Steven, five, and Joy, three, are going to the store with their mother. Both shout, "I want the front seat!" Mother says, "Come on, we're all one family and love each other." Joy kicks Steven. "Don't do that, Joy—Steven has rights just like you do. We have to respect each other!" Steven hits Joy in the mouth with his toy robot, R2D2. It's made of metal and it hurts! "Stop that or you'll both go to bed early tonight!" Joy and Steven are tearing at each other's clothes and screaming at the top of their lungs.

Mother calls off the trip to the store and calls her husband at work. "What am I going to do with these kids? I can't take them anywhere! I'm at the end of my rope! They won't listen to reason." Father comes home that evening, spanks Steven and Joy, opens a beer, and beats a retreat to the peace and quiet of his workbench in the garage. Mother is in her room crying. Neither Joy nor Steven know why they were spanked; they've long forgotten the incident.

Of course Mother realized that both her youngsters wanted to sit in the front seat—to be close to her and to feel big up there in front. But just knowing what's behind the fighting doesn't tell her what to do. If she continues to try to reason with her three- and five-year-old children as if they're miniature adults who understand the principles of a democratic society, they'll most likely continue dealing with each other at the most primitive level, i.e., physical fighting. She and her husband will begin to find themselves more and more disappointed and angry with each other.

Her problem is that she is talking to the kids in a "foreign language" they don't understand. It might have been better if she'd simply *put* Steven and R2D2 in the back seat to ride there together and left Joy in the front. Why? "Because I say so."

A family with young children, as I've said before, is not a democracy. It just isn't. It must deal with unequal power among the members. Power is an undeniable fact of life. And that power needs to be used—responsibly. After first taking action, Mother could *then* have made a special effort to talk to Steven and R2D2 as they drove to the store and reversed the seating on the way home a short time later. Of course, this would have to be done before the fighting escalated. But the children would realize something important: that Mother is bigger and more powerful than they are and makes the final decisions. And they would have learned that there *is* a better way: taking turns—a lesson *she* practiced for them.

Are They Progressing or Regressing?

Youngsters normally progress through stages in their capacity to understand and deal with the constant everyday problems between them. They need you to supply behavior control and decision making during their early years because they can't yet solve the problems alone. If this "outside" control from you is consistent and predictable, it eventually gets adopted and taken "inside" by them—it becomes self-control. Then rules of behaving and higher forms of negotiation—even cooperation—emerge. But you must know each level they're in when they're in it and adjust your approach to fit it; don't ask them to jump ahead several stages and think at a much higher level about how people get along with each other.

What are these stages of development like? Well, think about the seasons of the year. You dress your youngsters in one set of clothes for spring, another for summer, another for fall, another for winter. You wouldn't put a ski jacket on your son in the summer or a bikini on your daughter in the winter. Of course we know that seasons are not clear-cut—they overlap. Sometimes they go back and forth; then you get Indian summer or a spring snowstorm. But in general they're predictable. You know how to anticipate and respond to them.

You also know that, in addition to dressing your children for the season, you have to find new clothes for them every year or so because they grow so rapidly physically. It's harder to keep in mind that they're growing emotionally and mentally, too. Just as they grow out of clothes, they grow out of certain ways of thinking and behaving. When you buy new clothes for them, you most likely get them a little bit too large so they can grow into them.

The same thing goes for emotional stages of development. You wouldn't buy clothes several sizes too large. It would be just as silly to ask them to behave several sizes beyond the stage of growth their personality is in right now. But a "little bit of room to grow" doesn't hurt, so you can influence their progress to the next stage of development. That includes *talking* things out instead of fighting them out.

You not only have the influence to move them along; you may be able to speed them up a bit, too. Once again, it's important to recognize that brothers and sisters must go through a natural sequence from the early crude striking out at each other, through a stage of more sophisticated competition, and finally to a stage of collaboration.

In other words, you can help your children "outgrow" the enormous jealousies and envies of the early years when they feel they need to own everything in sight, including their parents, all by themselves, and don't want to share one drop of affection with each other. To them it feels as if only limited quantities are available, that there may not be enough to go around. No wonder they fight for it!

"Understanding" a brother or a sister's point of view develops very, very gradually; only in later years does empathy begin to erode the sharpness of rivalry and jealousy. First, kids have to learn to understand themselves. It will come if parents move along at the youngster's own developmental pace, working at a level he or she understands, at the same time showing the advantage of the next stage: "I guess I'll just have to *make* you kids stop fighting. But it would be much better if you stopped yourselves so we could get to the store and all the good things they have to eat there."

Perhaps most important, children can get stuck in an early stage and never move on if parents don't respond reasonably and progressively to their present capacity and also their future potential for dealing with each other. We've seen how demanding "too much, too soon" from Steven and Joy led to frustration and futility. If it continued, it might even prevent the development of a higher level of brother-sister relationship.

"Too little, too late" can do the same thing. If their mother had ignored them completely and let them "fight it out" over and over, she wouldn't have encouraged their progress either. Joy and Steven might very well grow up fighting not only with each other over every little thing, but with friends, too, and later on in life with colleagues at work and their own spouses. If it isn't managed and controlled at home, it spreads like a brush fire!

We all know people who are physically grown-up but remain bitterly competitive and rivalrous toward everyone they meet. This may sometimes work in the tough world of business, but not with friends and family. These people rarely have good friendships that last. Their marriages are hot and cold, on and off. It's as if part of them is still a little child who feels helpess and has to win over someone else to feel good or loved. They're still fighting early battles with younger brothers or sisters. Only now the battles have been transferred to adults.

So your job as a parent is to help young, unformed personalities gradually to "outgrow" sibling rivalry and begin to get along. It's useless to hope they will suddenly, magically, "grow out of it."

A *Matter of Life and Death!*

Steven, ten, and Joy, now eight, were learning to play checkers with each other. But the games were never finished. Whoever was losing would accuse the other of cheating. The board would be overturned amid shouting and accusations. Checkers suddenly changed their function. They became missiles and flew all over the room! Father, exasperated, was tempted to send the kids to their rooms after a good spanking. But he remembered a conversation he and his wife had had at breakfast.

"They're just like people at a cocktail party," she said. "First they don't know each other and act cool and reserved, then for a while things warm up and go well, but if the party goes on too long, they can't handle it and things go to pieces."

He noticed that the kids had been bored and started the game in a friendly way. Now they were in the middle. One began to get ahead of the other. Clearly someone was going to win and someone lose. Things were getting out of hand, but they hadn't gone too far yet. Maybe they could be saved!

Father noticed they were still in a "talking mood." (Once a child is beyond this, in a temper tantrum or shouting "everyone is against me!" forget reasoning—act decisively to terminate the discussion.) So he decided to try something.

"You guys both seem to have to win all the time," he

said. "That's not the way checkers is. Someone wins sometimes and someone loses."

Joy: "But he'll always win. He's older!"

Father: "Not if you use a handicap. It takes a long time
and a lot of practice to get better at checkers. It doesn't
happen at once. I used to lose all the time when I was first
learning. Here, let me play each of you once and see what
the difference is and then you can start over with Steven
having a few less checkers. Then it's more even and you'll
each win sometimes and lose sometimes."

Steven: "But that's not fair! I'm bigger and I should
win—she's stupid!"

Father: "She's just younger than you are, Steven. I
guess you'd be embarrassed if your little sister beat you—
but not if it's even to start with. You volunteer to give up
some strength; it's not taken from you. You both seem
scared to lose to the other guy, as if it's life or death and
the loser gets killed! Here, let me play a game with each of
you. We'll see how much difference there is between you
and I'll try to teach you both some good plays at the same
time."

Father not only showed them the meaning of victory and
defeat, he showed them how to play and some strategy of his
own. Each would watch how the other played against him and
root for the other to win. The kids were temporarily unlocked
from battle. They were in a truce until they could see the value
of adopting a new set of rules. Then there'd be a fresh start
with Father as referee.

Steven knew if he acted that way with his friends they
wouldn't play with him. But this was his younger sister, of all
people! He couldn't let her beat him! He might lose his seniority in the household. But Dad was giving him a way out, a way
to save face. Now checkers could become a game, not a
fight for survival. And the frustration of Joy, the underdog
who really wanted to take over because she didn't like being

younger, was defused and she got a chance to learn to be a better player, too.

Your children need to achieve a degree of self-confidence that doesn't depend on beating others to maintain itself. The key is to know the stage your child is in and its characteristics, to realize that it's a normal developmental stage, to show him or her the next higher level and the advantages of advancing into it.

Let's discuss the stages and I'll show you what I mean.

Phases of Sibling Relationships—An Overview of the Four Commandments

When youngsters are very young, they obey to avoid punishment. Who is boss is the most important question. This is the Might Equals Right stage, when the child's favorite phrase is "That's mine!" and the parents' is "This hurts me more than it hurts you" (which is hardly ever true).

Following this dog-eat-dog period between brothers and sisters in the preschool years, there's a shift toward partial control over fighting—a mutually agreed upon truce held together by the flimsy principle You Scratch My Back and I'll Scratch Yours. It's a period of enlightened self-interest. Later, things do begin to change into the wish for parents' approval, so they behave, or at least they behave sufficiently to avoid disapproval.

We can call this stage No Fair Cheating or The Law and Order Stage because it emphasizes rules to insure fairness for everyone and keep things under control. It marks a truly significant milestone in growing up because youngsters can now manage things among themselves. If everyone has agreed to the same rule, they no longer need adults (except occasionally when things fall apart) to act as policemen at their shoulders all the time. Finally, this Law and Order orientation (the level at which most people in our society largely operate from day to day) can, in some youngsters, evolve even further. It needs a real conscience with its own values which keeps an older youngster from taking unfair advantage of a younger one because it's more than unfair, it's not right.

No longer is disapproval by a parent (or even a member of one's own age group) the deterrent. It's the need to avoid *self*-disapproval. This final stage, the fourth commandment of sibling relations, is rarely openly acknowledged. That would be expecting too much. It's most often grudgingly expressed as As Brothers and Sisters Go, You're Not So Bad.

Let's look at the stages in order.

MIGHT EQUALS RIGHT

Let's face it. Preschool youngsters are basically self-centered. They think the world revolves around them and everything in it belongs to them. Total selfishness is the starting point in life and quite normal. Children at this age quite naturally want their parents to themselves. Anyone else, *especially* a brother or a sister, is an intruder and therefore an enemy (people in a small child's mind are divided into friends and enemies, good and bad).

The favorite slogan "That's mine!" looms even bigger at special times such as the birth of a new brother or sister into the family or at Christmas. Yes, sadly enough, jealousy and fighting over toys reaches its peak in the season of giving. (See the section "The Christmas Holidays" in Chapter IV.)

It often seems that property or things are more important than people to youngsters during this period. It's as if a kid's status depends on having more or better possessions, as if the physical properties of toys are taken on by their owner. "His balloon is bigger than my balloon" (they're the same size). Steven wants a *bigger* ball than Joy's doll. Expense doesn't matter; it's size that counts!

Size is applied to people, too. In a world where the reality is unequal power, big people are more powerful than little people. Like it or not, this is the level where you have to meet the child because it's the level he or she understands—and for the most visible reason. Youngsters feel small and helpless because they see grown-ups as big and powerful beings who not only control *how* and *why* things happen but decide *what* things happen; they seem to own the whole world.

Steven announces to the kids on the block: "My Daddy's got the biggest car in the world!" (It may be a subcompact.) And so power and bigness are interpreted by very young children as *the* critical factor in human relationships.

Limited though it may be, this orientation toward Might Equals Right is real and needs to be responded to. It's why discipline becomes crucial. It's another fact of life: children don't develop their own internal control for some time—not until they're exposed to reasonable external controls from you, controls that had best become absolutely predictable over time.

I'll Count to Three

Steven and Joy loved to play with blocks. They'd gotten a big set for Christmas and spent the whole afternoon making things—houses, roads, buildings. It was amazing how they could play so well for so long. That evening, just before bedtime, the blocks were still strewn all over the floor. Mother decided to give him a few minutes' warning and asked them to start picking up.

Joy cried, "No, it's not time for bed!" Steven screamed, "They're her blocks! She did it!" The argument began to deteriorate. "You did!" "I didn't!" Mother decided to call a halt: "Okay, kids, you've got till the count of three to begin picking up the blocks together since I saw you both playing with them. If you can't do it by then, there'll be no bedtime story tonight."

Both children sulked. No blocks were picked up and there was no bedtime story. Mother picked them up afterward, gritted her teeth, and resolved to keep trying. The next night and several nights afterward the count of 1-2-3 worked. They both rushed to get to work picking up. They didn't do the most efficient job, but they did it. A few nights later, Mother said, "Okay, kids, time to get ready for bed!" Joy said, "Come on, Steven, we've got till the count of three!"

Joy and Steven realized that Mother was persistent and consistent. She wasn't going to change, so they'd better. Joy adopted Mother's early warning system of counting to three herself, so it didn't have to come from Mother anymore. It became her own early version of a *conscience*. Instead of keeping up a pointless squabble over who ought to do the work, she began to assume some responsibility of her own with only the hint of a warning from outside.

If things continued this way, you could expect that eventually the children would pick things up themselves without having to be told, or with minimal argument. If Mother had decided it was easier to pick things up herself, particularly when the children fought over whose responsibility it was, or if she had taken sides with one against the other or hadn't given them a "face-saving" warning, their lack of responsibility for their own behavior would have continued and problems would likely have mounted.

The corollary to this first commandment of living—Might Equals Right—is that the child wants to avoid punishment. If you decide to give up being number one (and grabbing toys from your brother or sister) to feel big and strong, it's to avoid punishment from Daddy because he's bigger and can't be fooled around with as a little brother or sister can.

Punishment, by the way, is *not* a bad word! You don't have to be ashamed to use it. Ordinarily it's a necessary part of discipline, which is an essential ingredient for growing up. (See the section "Forms of Discipline to Use for Fighting" in this chapter.)

How discipline is given—that's the crucial issue. If a parent is always cold and critical, his or her discipline won't be effective. What's to be gained by obeying if you never get any warmth or affection anyway?

If physical punishment is the first, not the last, resort, if it's too severe to absorb and to learn from, it becomes a matter of passing on the punishment to somebody else, especially one who is smaller. To be effective, discipline must be consistent, with both parents agreeing to make mutual decisions. If they use differing styles youngsters will be confused.

This doesn't mean parents always have to decide everything together. Problems that need dealing with should be dealt with at that moment, not postponed "until Daddy comes home" because then they're meaningless to a young child who can't remember what happened two hours ago. General agreement about the use of various kinds of discipline—isolation, deprivation, and physical punishment—is more important than whether you err from time to time either on the too strict or too lenient side. If both parents are on the strict side or both on the lenient side (within reasonable bounds), it's less confusing for a youngster than if one is always very strict and the other is always very lenient.

It's also important that punishment be reasonable: don't send little Shirley to the electric chair for a misdemeanor or let Tommy off with a warning for a felony! Excessive control (such as physical punishment used routinely) usually develops when control has been ineffective. Insecure and frightened parents establish highly restrictive controls. If they're comfortable with their own ability to be firm but reasonable, the children usually pick this up and get along more smoothly.

Probably the best discipline for fighting is separation and brief isolation: a parental response that merely deals with the *fact* of the fighting, rather than trying to find out all the ins and outs of it. It's often difficult, if not impossible, to find the real culprit. Mutual provoking between brothers and sisters goes on over a long time and defies identification of its parts except for occasional flash points which really may be small segments of the whole story. Usually sending each child to his or her room for a brief time will suffice to teach a lesson, and teaching a lesson is the only real justification for discipline.

Deprivation of privileges, if reasonable and short, is also an effective discipline-learning device. Let's see how they can be combined with an introduction to the next higher stage, You Scratch My Back and I'll Scratch Yours.

Some Days It Feels Like Armageddon

Father is reading the paper and young Joy is watching Bugs Bunny on television. Steven wants to change the channel to Batman. He changes it. Joy cries. Through her tears, she slaps him. He hits her with a block. It all happened so fast Father wasn't able to prevent it, so he dives in when a two-way temper tantrum of gigantic proportions has erupted. He carries both to their rooms.

After ten minutes, when they seem to have calmed down, he invites them back to the living room to help decide how the television is to be divided. But no one is in a listening mood. A resumption of the cartoon program results in trouble, mainly subtle poking and pushing by Steven.

Now Father says the television will be turned off and will stay off for the evening. Steven is very angry and kicks the television set. He's sent to bed early. Father says, "Steven, you kept acting up all evening long, so I had to stop you. So I did because I have to decide what goes on here and how far things can go. But that's not the way I like to do things. I'd much rather have played a game with you or read you an extra bedtime story if you'd let Joy leave her cartoon on."

Kissing Joy good night, he says, "I know you were watching Bugs Bunny, but if you'd have done Steven a favor by letting him watch Batman, his favorite program,

I'll bet he'd have given you your choice next time. Standing up for your rights is okay, but giving in to your brother to avoid a fight might be even more fun because next time he would owe you a favor."

Once a real tantrum has begun, as I've said, there's no point in trying to reason or even talk to a preschooler. He or she simply needs to be isolated and have time to cool off. You can't always catch trouble early. Once the air has been cleared you can try again. Here, Father matter-of-factly intervenes and stops the fighting. He does it with a comfortable authority, not overreacting by being excessively punitive and not ignoring it, hoping for the impossible—that two preschoolers can "learn to settle things themselves." But then he goes a step beyond merely settling it at the level of the preschooler's thinking and expectations. He shows them the advantages of working toward a better settlement. He suggests that doing favors for other people will get you what you want more often than fighting for it. For the kids, this is a new principle. They can't understand it yet. But they're given a "preview of coming attractions."

YOU SCRATCH MY BACK AND I'LL SCRATCH YOURS

During the early grade school years, youngsters slowly shift from an orientation toward force and power and avoidance of punishment as the first commandment of living, to the second, a practical hedonism or enlightened self-interest, a realization that you have to give a little to get the things you want. Often an armed truce can be negotiated based on favor exchange. "Doing unto others as you would have them do unto you" is a salable principle in the early years—not because it's moral but because you're more likely to get what you want out of life that way if you live and let live.

To be really effective, it has to develop between brothers and sisters themselves. But parents can start it off. "You kids stop bugging each other and we'll make chocolate chip cookies" may sound like a "bribe," and the principle is sometimes rejected by parents because they don't want to be "blackmailed." But there is a time when you can best respond to a child's wish to get what he or she wants with trade-offs. It's a simple unwritten contract or agreement between two parties, even if they don't completely trust each other.

The SALT agreement between our country and Russia is very complicated. But it boils down to a very simple principle—we'll each have only a certain same number of each kind of missile and then permit inspection because everyone knows you can't trust the Russians (or the Americans). It's better than nothing and we'll see if it works; then maybe we can go a step further.

Most important of all, brothers and sisters are likely to begin to use it with each other. It's the favor-exchange principle at work: each builds a bank account of favors with others through negotiation. Empathy and altruism come later. You do have to go through the first stage to get to the second.

It's really a temporary stage of human relations. If someone does a favor for you, you have an obligation. It may not get at the root cause of sibling rivalry, but it begins to reduce the intensity—fighting to have everything or just more than someone else. It's a shift away from punishment-avoidance as the primary motivation for civilized behavior. It uses the youngster's own motivation to begin the change from pure selfishness to learning ways for dealing with others. So don't be afraid to use it temporarily. Parents who stick to physical punishment because they're afraid of being blackmailed in the "favor stage" are often the ones who complain the loudest that their children continue to fight longer than others!

"You Love Him More Than Me!"

Steven is now eight and Joy is six. Steven: "Mommy, why is she always coming into my room and playing with my models? She breaks 'em! Girls don't know anything about models! Why do they want to play with 'em anyway?" Mother: "Steven, Joy just told me the same thing about you going into her room for crayons and paper. Maybe the two of you can agree that she won't come into your room if you don't go into hers. At least it's a start."

Of course, Joy goes into Steven's room three days later. She has forgotten the deal. Naturally, Mother is discouraged. But she reminds herself that progress isn't a straight line. For every step forward, you can expect one backward. Should she give each of them a cabinet to lock their things in? That's one way, and it's fine as a temporary solution. But it won't move the kids to a higher level of dealing with each other. It will keep them on a "cold war" footing. Mother will have to be the United Nations peacekeeping force, patrolling the demilitarized zone and watching for violations into forbidden territory. So she decides that some kind of discipline is indicated. After all, Steven has kept his end of the bargain. Joy is younger and therefore more likely to slip back, testing to see if she can get her way when she wants it.

When Mother tells her she can't go next door to play that afternoon, Joy screams, "You don't love me!"

Mother hugs her to show that she does, but a deal is a deal.

"Well, you love Steven more than me! I can tell!"

Mother: "I know that's the way you feel right now, and you used to feel that way a lot more when you were little. Mommy and Daddy love you and Steven very much. We loved you a lot when you were born, and we love you even more as you're growing up. But some of that has to be earned. You have to work for it if it's to keep growing bigger. And one of the ways of getting more love and other things is by not fighting with Steven and keeping your part of the bargain."

Mother is explaining to Joy the concept that it pays to

please her by working things out with Steven, because a three-way exchange of favors builds a bank account of love.

Again, this phase is only a way station. The trick is to shed old ways of dealing with each other as the limitations become obvious—much as a snake sheds its skin—and to allow for growth into new and better ways—again at the pace of the youngster's own emotional development.

Besides repeating and reinforcing one pattern (e.g., You Scratch My Back and I'll Scratch Yours) over and over for a year or two, you can also begin to show the advantages of moving on into a phase where rules are set for their own sake, where adults don't have to be on watch because a system of law and order is operating.

"You Always Get More Than Me!"

Steven and Joy are now ten and eight. Joy: "Grandma took Steven to the movies for the second time in a row!' Steven shouts back: "You were having a birthday party!" Joy: "I set the table for you last night." Steven is incensed. He can't lose this battle. "So what? I loaned you my warm-up jacket!" Joy figures she'll get the last word: "But you owed me a favor because of last Christmas." This incredible generalization inspires Steven to new heights: "I didn't either! And besides, you got to play my records at your birthday party."

Every good system of favors breaks down. Don't try to prop it up and keep it going forever. Look toward the next stage and show the advantages of it.

Mother's been listening and realizes it's time to intervene. She has to referee again. Maybe she should get a black and white striped shirt and a whistle. Lately the kids have been working things out better by themselves, but now it's time to bring out the whistle. Football players can handle the game by themselves for only so long. Then their emotions get the better of them and the fouls explode.

She says, "You kids are impossible! I've been keeping score. You both have three points. You're even. Now why don't you try to work out some rules that get you out of this, just like I've seen you do playing games with your friends out in the backyard? I'll help if you want me to."

IT'S NOT FAIR, YOU'RE CHEATING—THE LAW AND ORDER STAGE

We've now pretty much passed through the first orientation of young children when parental authority is really the only reliable control over relations between brothers and sisters. And we've passed through a phase of learning that one can earn favors from someone else, improve one's own situation, and get what one wants. In the later grade school years, they're ready to move a step further. They can agree on rules and agree to abide by them even when it hurts (because the rule goes against you).

Joy and Steven can now make a firm rule with each other that each will not go into the other's room without permission. They can even allow that violations are inevitable, spelling out penalties—part of the precious weekly allowance, doing all the chores for a day, etc. They can play games together because there's an imaginary third party they both accept, the rule book. They can refer to it when there's a dispute. And usually one reluctantly gives in, as long as the other doesn't take unfair advantage and rub it in with too much laughing and enjoyment of winning the argument.

The rule book is valuable for its own sake. Ideas of fairness and justice become acceptable, especially if parents have encouraged them. They promote and maintain a social order within a youngster's own small world, replacing the purely

physical consequences of behavior, the dependence on a balance of power, or even the selfish orientation toward matching
one's own wishes against a brother or sister's.

"I Get the Bathroom First!"

Steven and Joy are twelve and ten. Each likes to take
a shower after dinner. Steven complains, "Joy spends an
hour in there and uses up all the hot water!"

Joy angrily counters, "You leave your clothes all over
the floor! Besides, you run to get there first while I'm still
finishing my part in the kitchen cleanup."

Steven shouts: "That's because I'm faster than you!
Girls are slow! That's why they're always late; even Dad
says that about Mom."

Joy screams, "You're a male chauvinist pig-face!"

At this point, Mother says as calmly as she can, "I've
noticed that both of you have been having trouble over
the bathroom, fighting over it a lot. You've got a rule
about not going into each other's room without permission. Can you make up some rules about the bathroom?"

Joy: "Sure, you can't leave it a mess with your clothes
all over; that's rule number one."

Steven: "That's okay with me if there's a time limit on
how long you can be in there. And you can't turn on the
hot water and just let it run for twenty minutes."

Joy: "Okay, how about half an hour time limit?"

Steven: "Okay, that's rule number two, but how about
who goes first?" Steven, who's older, still has a bit of an
edge on Joy when it comes to willingness to invent and
live by rules. This can be to her advantage—if she agrees
to his rule and finds, to her surprise, that she's protected
by it and even gets better access to the bathroom. Steven
suggests they each alternate a week of going first and
there are certain times you're assigned the bathroom;

, to pick seven-thirty. They draw up a schedule and
to the bathroom door.

u can see, a little gear shifting by parents allowed the
youngsters to work out their own rules. They're now ready to
share equally, based on what's "fair." It's not just a matter
of reciprocity. The accepted fact is that there has to be "law
and order" and that each has a commitment to respect the
law. They don't even need penalties very often anymore. Yet,
they've actually made a commitment to a new basis for dealing
with people. And it's the way most of the world operates.

Unfortunately "law and order" has gotten a bad name in
recent years because it was used for the wrong reasons. A
presidential administration was even facetiously labeled the
"law and order administration" because of its use and abuse of
the concept. Still, it's an honorable concept. It reflects individual responsibility, the conventional morality that it pays
to be "good" in order to get the approval of others. Getting
approval is a step beyond avoiding disapproval. Being "nice"
to others, including brothers and sisters, becomes possible.

All the previous stages (Might Equals Right, You Scratch
My Back and I'll Scratch Yours) have come together with
No Fair Cheating to produce this new level of behavior.

Earlier rivalries between brothers and sisters may still
smolder but they're less intense because the kids are "branch-
ing out" from the family. They direct some of their aggressive
and competitive feelings toward other age mates and channel
them into teams, games, and sports. They form cliques—friendships with two and three children. These are the relationships
of importance. Minor quarrels and new rivalries for best friends
become subjects of dinner table conversations.

Rules of the game become very important. Youngsters are
exquisitely sensitive to issues that invoke fairness, justice, and

loyalty, partly because they're just learning to accept rules and control their own selfish impulses. Anyone who's going to subordinate his or her own wishes to the needs of the group will be suspicious that *others* are cheating to get what they want; its tough to control your own wishes. They'd still like to get what they want.

So a good part of the old competition gets deflected from the family setting into a more socially acceptable form, with one team trying to win against another. In individual sports, golf and tennis, you see how strictly the rules are enforced. You're supposed to call *yourself* for a rule violation, not rely on a referee or opponent.

Think about tennis for a minute. It's really the only sport constantly demanding close judgment calls that win or lose points for yourself. This fits the intense need of youngsters between eight and twelve for things to be exactly fair. They often call close-to-the-line shots against themselves if they're uncertain—and not simply because other people might be watching. Their own conscience is watching! A youngster who calls them "out" when they're "in" more than once or twice finds it hard to get partners. There's usually no referee or umpire to blame for "bad calls." You have to blame yourself and live with yourself.

Bad News Bears

The Pirates were playing the Yankees in the finals of the district Little League championship. The ninth inning. Score tied at 15–15. The go-ahead run on third for the Pirates. A ground ball to second. It's bobbled. Throw to home. Steven slides in and is called out on a very, very close play. The Yankees go on to win it, 16–15, in the last of the ninth.

Steven's father has been having a fit in the stands and trying to arouse all the Pirates' parents. The umpire had called his son out at home plate! "He was safe by a mile;

the umpire was blocked out and couldn't see. I think we should appeal." Steven and his teammates are broken-hearted, but Steven, through his tears, whispers, "Dad, he was right, I was out. I felt the tag before I touched the plate. You've got to play fair."

Grade school is the time for parents to encourage team participation. Involvement in team sports is especially important for brothers and sisters who've been the most intensely competitive at home. They need to channel it into outside activities and have the support of a group so they can "learn to lose." Somehow it's not so bad if others lose with you; you're not alone.

It's a time when parents should encourage team participation. It is constructive competition and it pays off. The destructive competition at home often goes down almost in direct proportion to team involvement. You need to attend games to show your approval and support.

Little League brings many problems. The competition may get too intense, largely because of poor coaching or over-involved parents (as in the case of Steven's father). Parents seem to get so caught up that winning is more important for them than it is for the youngsters. But the kids are learning something besides winning: winning and losing go together—if you're going to win, you're going to lose sometimes too.

This push toward fairness and sticking to the rules comes from within, from a new way of looking at the world. Brothers and sisters who've lived by the "law of survival" (whoever is bigger, older, or smarter rules those underneath) realize that this state only produces a constant state of tension. If you're always looking over your shoulder to see who's going to belt you next, you don't have much time or energy left to have fun. So having a "third party"—rules to govern dealings between people—seems a better way.

This inner drive to get away from the law of the jungle needs outside support—support from you—to grow and become a habit, a part of one's self. It's very important that the grown-ups who serve as models reinforce it by sticking to rules themselves. Guess what happens when they don't?

Safe at First (A True Story)

Millions of youngsters were watching the World Series on television. It was a critical game. The Yankees had a rally going. If they could win this game, they still had a chance. A ground ball to second. One out. The throw to first. The ball bounced off the hip of the Yankee runner into right field and he was ruled safe. The rally continued and the Yankees won the game. And the series.

The ruling was: "If the runner is accidentally hit, he's safe. If he intentionally got in the way of the ball, he's out." The television announcers, former baseball greats themselves, used the miraculous instant replay and various angles to show over and over again that the runner actually moved *out* of the baseline and into the path of the ball, deflecting it. But the umpire wasn't in a position to see it. Chuckling over and over as they replayed the scene, the announcers said to each other, "Isn't he clever? Well, there's nothing wrong if you can get away with it!"

Television sports are watched by millions of youngsters who identify themselves with favorite teams and heroes. One of the most important influences on them is the philosophy of the announcers. Throughout the football season, their secret weapon, the instant replay from various angles, shows obvious fouls by defensive players that the referees miss, offensive players cheating and then denying it, everyone in the pileup fighting for a "fumble" after the whistle blows the play dead.

The enjoyment of players "getting away with" rule violations and not being caught has become, for some announcers, a prominent part of their telecast. For the millions of youngsters watching, it's confusing. Their fragile conscience, with its

standards of right and wrong just emerging, needs outside re-
inforcement if it's to keep developing. When grown-ups,
especially sports heroes, undermine the preadolescent thirst
for justice and fair play it produces emotional damage at least
as serious as physical injuries because it is more widespread.

At home, interest in games as a more civilized form of
competition also increases. But it's one thing to channel
brother and sister energies into team sports outdoors; it's another for siblings to confront each other over a board game
at home!

Scooble Is Not a Word!

Steven and Joy were playing Scrabble. It was the first
time in days they seemed to be enjoying each other. But
ten or fifteen minutes of friendly competition in a game
is about all that school age brothers and sisters can handle.
Steven shouted, "There's no such word as 'scooble'!" Joy
countered, "Yes, there is! I saw it in the comics last
week." Steven: "You're a dirty cheater." Joy: "You can't
call me that, stupid!"

Just as Joy was getting ready to yank Steven's hair,
Mother said, "I'll bet she did see it in the comics. There
are lots of words like that in the funny papers. But how
did you agree to decide whether a word is real or not for
this game?" Steven and Joy shouted together: "The
dictionary." The game resumed.

Sometimes parents need to make the rules and also act as
impartial referees to enforce them. At other times, they can
quickly help youngsters over a hurdle. Here Joy and Steven
were beginning to fight over a game. The fact that it's a
higher level of wanting to win than, say, one having better
toys than the other is small comfort when the kids are fighting
over rules and shouting "cheater!"

Mother realized there is always a back-and-forth oscillation from earlier behavior to the current higher levels, gradual progress marked by occasional slips backward. All she needed to do was to reorient them from greed back to fairness. She'll need to do this over and over again, with injections of "fairness reminders" whenever peace begins to fall apart.

Card games or board games bring direct confrontation between brothers and sisters. That's very different from the indirect displacement of their competition into team sports, where opponents serve as "substitutes" for themselves. So at home it's often important for parents to dilute this direct confrontation. It may be too much for the kids to handle. You can help by encouraging the involvement of several people, including yourselves, in a game, rather than just letting children play by themselves. This takes the sharp edge off a one-to-one, win-or-lose situation which inevitably arouses old jealousies and hostilities. They may have buried the hatchet—but it gets dug up again over and over.

You can also help control strife by carefully selecting the games you buy for your youngsters. Don't just buy a game because it's new and exciting looking. Size it up. Some games emphasize a skill that will produce one winner over and over. Avoid that kind. The required skill might be the ability to calculate arithmetically, good coordination between the eye and hand movements, or the ability to imagine and create words. Such games will lock your youngsters into a pattern of one being superior based on the particular skill called for. You can bet there'll be fighting.

Even the old game of jacks is risky. Age difference means coordination difference, and jacks emphasizes coordination. It's often better to choose games that are just fun to play, games with less emphasis on the outcome. Or choose some with chance or luck as a major factor, i.e., where the dice are rolled and eventually decide the winner. (See the section "Games and Toys" in Chapter IV.)

How do we move beyond rigid adherence to rules? Watch.

Go Directly to Jail, Do Not Pass Go
(But Go on to the Next Stage)

The family was playing Monopoly on a rainy Sunday afternoon. After a while, it was clear that the kids used very different strategies—strategies that would eventually eliminate both of them from the game because they were too narrow and limited. Joy was only interested in sinking all her money in a few selected properties, especially Park Place and Boardwalk, and building them up with as many hotels as possible. If somebody landed on Park Place before she did, she would plead, "Please don't buy it. I want it. I'll give you anything if you let me have it!" She seemed sure that these glamorous places held special magic and she ignored that she'd sooner or later be caught short and lose the game before they could pay off.

Of course, this gave her brother, Steven, an enormous weapon. But his strategy, besides teasing his sister, was to accumulate and hoard as much money as possible. He didn't consider the odds either: that in the long run he was bound to lose. He just wanted to satisfy his greed and have more money than anyone else.

Mother was playing a more balanced game and was winning. (This was tolerable to both children just as long as one of them wasn't.)

Steven passed Go and took $400 from the bank. Joy cried, "You're cheating; you only get $200 for passing Go. I caught you." Steven, whose shoulder was bent double from the heavy chip it was carrying, defensively growled, "I forgot to take it the last time I went around, so I'm just making up for it this time."

Father intervened just before the board was overturned: "Okay, kids, let's check the rule book on that. If there isn't a rule that specifically deals with it, we'll have to decide together because it could happen over

and over again in lots of ways. How about it, Steven?"
Steven: "Well, I guess it isn't right. Forget the rule book,
Dad, we don't need it."

On the one hand, the kids wanted to win so much they
developed narrow strategies merely to defeat the other. This
rarely leads to success; only occasionally. When the tension
mounted and a quarrel began they agreed to settle it by going
back to the rule book. Then a curious thing happened. Steven's
father was able to encourage Steven to stretch a bit and reach
a higher level of settling an argument with his sister. He gave
in to her because of *moral principle*, a new development just
ready to hatch.

AS BROTHERS AND SISTERS GO, YOU'RE NOT SO BAD

Most of society operates on a day-to-day basis in the third
(Law and Order) stage. For many it becomes the philosophy
of life. A more advanced stage is more or less developed in
some adolescents. It creeps up on them in high school and is
marked by the development of a set of moral principles to live
by. They remain important all by themselves and don't depend
on what friends think or a group code. They have value in
themselves. The rights of other people are understood and
supported.

This stage can be encouraged by parents, but watch out:
don't try too early, not before they're ready. If you see it emerge
from the sequence of stages I've described, you'll find brother-
and-sister fighting becomes rare. (Steven had outgrown the
"legalistic" emphasis of law and order, the rule book stage.)
And you don't develop it by moralizing or lecturing to them.
It happens only if development has moved along well from
one stage to the next and the kids now can see what had been
there all along—a family value: emphasis on respect for others
and not taking advantage. Parents show this in their relationship with each other and the way they talk about the people
they work with. Children listen and learn.

If brothers and sisters do begin to show genuine respect for each other, don't expect them to admit it openly. Don't rub their noses in it! The best you can expect is for them to admit grudgingly that *their* brother or sister really isn't so bad after all, compared to others they know!

Sibling Rivalry: Going, Going. . . ?

Steven, seventeen, had a bad cold. He and his sister Joy, fifteen, had household chores which they alternated weekly. This week Joy was setting the table and taking out the trash. It was Steven's week to help with the dishes. Just a few months before, they had renegotiated the chores, each complaining about having the worst of the bargain, but deciding to make up their own rules of rotation and division of labor. They had stuck to them with a few reminders by Mom and Dad.

Steven had the flu and hardly ate any dinner. Afterward Joy said, "Why don't you go to bed, Steven? You don't look so hot. I'll do the dishes." Steven: "Thanks, sis! You sure *you're* not the one who's sick?"

Joy didn't even ask for a favor in return. She went beyond her usual ways of dealing with Steven—based on contracts and obligations. She remembered how she'd felt when she had the flu and put herself in her brother's shoes. Empathy, a capacity for understanding other people's problems and points of view, had hatched.

Children really can't picture how other people feel when they're younger. First they have to understand and master their own feelings. Capacity for empathy can emerge in the teens but needs cultivating. Steven and Joy's parents always showed concern for each other. Joy had noticed this and also that they didn't take advantage of each other. Her orientation shifted toward what was "right" as a basis for getting along with Steven. The golden rule now had real meaning. She'd moved beyond operating by the letter of the law.

Parents can help develop an understanding of other points of view by asking how the kids think someone else feels. If you do this over and over again, especially when someone has been hurt, empathy will develop. When it does, you can confidently allow youngsters to work out their own problems together. You no longer have to be involved; the era of rivalry is over.

As I've said earlier, sibling rivalry often surprises and perplexes parents. They hadn't expected the constant fighting. What happened to their ideal of a family with two or three children who lived happily together? You always thought brothers and sisters would love each other, right? But your kids seem to positively *hate* each other! (Actually, they're doing some of both, but it's hard for us to accept that two such opposite feelings can exist side by side.)

There aren't any magical solutions. You can't just stamp it out. But dealing with it can be a part of raising children that's challenging and rewarding. All you need to know is that it's normal and universal but can be outgrown. If that's to happen, you have to know how your children's mental and emotional capacities develop. You can't expect more than they can produce.

When youngsters are very young, they constantly try to decide who is boss. That's why they fight so much. They tend to obey only to avoid punishment. It's a very simple outlook on life. As we've seen, parents need to deal with children at that level to keep sibling competition and fighting under control, at the most peaceable level possible, and that means measured discipline. When youngsters move into the school years, they begin to shift and develop partial control over fighting through a truce held together by favor exchange ("You scratch my back and I'll scratch yours").

Later they shift further into wishing for approval, or at least into going along to avoid disapproval from parents.

Further progress comes with the discovery of rules to insure fairness to everyone and this developmental stream keeps flowing in the later grade school years. This is the Law and Order level where much of society operates. Conscience is a higher internal system of control which, as time goes along, can keep an older brother or sister from taking unfair advantage of a younger. Conscience development means that fighting is kept under control to avoid *self*-condemnation and because it's "not right" to take unfair advantage of someone else. But remember: don't try to build it too early. It has to be cultivated.

Youngsters move through these stages at varying speeds; they may be half in and half out of a particular stage or stop at any stage at any age. Remember: for every two steps forward, they take one backward. If they keep moving along, you can move with them, encouraging the development of the next stage. You have to know what that stage is and think of ways to bring it into everyday family relationships.

It's most important not to assume more from youngsters than they can give, not to deal with them as if they're more advanced than they are in the capacity to share and be fair. Knowing about these stages and their sequence can be the ultimate key to dealing with sibling rivalry in your family and coming out of it alive and even happy.

A Conversation About Discipline and Sibling Rivalry— Handling Everyday Problems

"That's all very fine," said one mother. "You've reassured me that they'll outgrow it if I keep on getting in tune with them as they grow up and help them move ahead. I realize I've got to work on it. But I need some more practical help for everyday situations and how to handle them. How to handle myself, too. In my *mind*, I know their fighting is normal. *Emotionally*, though, it gets to me. I lose my temper and blow up at them.

Sometimes I feel so guilty and inadequate because I can't control myself—or them! I want them to grow up to be friends *so* much."

"Of course you do. But you'll be amazed that too much urging and pushing friendship can backfire. If you treat them as separate, as different, they're more likely to become friends on their own. The main point right now is that you need to set limits and stick to them."

"But those newspaper columns for parents tell me that paying attention to the fighting actually reinforces it and makes it increase. They say I should ignore it so my boys will have a chance to learn to settle their battles on their own. I know that's true because, when my husband and I were away for a weekend and came home, our youngest, Peter, wasn't screeching anymore when his older brother hit him, and his older brother wasn't shouting 'He hit me first'. I asked them about it and they said the baby-sitter just ignored the screeching so they decided to go on and switch to something else."

"It's certainly true that if they know how to push your red button, they'll do it. Maybe their screeching is your red button. Perhaps you were sucked in and became overinvolved in that department. Being away for the weekend broke up a pattern because the baby-sitter handled it differently. One extreme is being overinvolved; the other extreme is totally ignoring the fighting. Would you just stand by and let them beat each other to a pulp? They need your help and guidance. It's your responsibility to set limits and provide discipline. You don't have to be an angel with a flaming sword who'll stamp the fighting out . . . you can't produce a miracle. Nobody can have two young boys who play beautifully together and love each other all the time."

"I'm still confused about when and how much and what kind of discipline to use. When is it harmful? I was always told that I shouldn't disapprove of my children; it's their *behavior* I'm supposed to disapprove of. How can you separate the two? If your children never feel disapproved of and always loved 'just the same' no matter what they've done, why have any motivation to behave?

"Take yesterday: Peter and Mark were flying Mark's new remote control model airplane in the driveway. Peter got mad because his older brother wouldn't let him handle it all by himself. He took the plane and smashed it on the ground. Mark socked him and I came running when he screamed. I told Peter it wasn't him I was angry at, it was what he *did*."

"Is that the way you really felt?"

"No, I felt he was being a little brat! And I was sore as a boil because he had broken the $24.95 airplane Mark had saved up for."

"Well, how can you separate Peter from what he did? Who did it? Some mysterious forces in the atmosphere? Did the plane fly over the Bermuda Triangle? No, Peter did it! Of course you were mad at him just as Mark was. It won't give him a trauma to know that. Maybe he needs to know that you *don't* love him just the same all the time. Why pretend if you don't? Give him some reason for trying to control himself and be accommodating to others' rights. One reason is not having you mad at him. Of course, there has to be enough basic affection between you and him so you can withdraw some of it from time to time and make your move effective. It's like a bank account. You open it for him with a deposit of a lot of love. When he's growing up, he needs to add to it by working for your approval. Maybe he should give up something as payment, a token, part of his allowance if he gets one. But don't take it away till the whole plane is paid for. He'll be old enough for high school then and long forgotten why he's being punished—he'll only think, *They don't like me.*"

"That's just it! I don't want him always feeling guilty like I did as a child."

"There's nothing wrong with *deserved* healthy guilt feelings when you've done something wrong as Peter did when he broke his brother's new model plane. It's only when you feel guilty all the time for no apparent reason that it's overdone. Peter

needs to be held responsible for his behavior. If you treat what
he did as if it were totally separate from him, it'll give him a
good excuse in the future for blaming things he does on
something or somebody else. But there *is* one kind of situation
when it's a good idea to disapprove of the *act*."

"What's that?"

"Lots of times you'll be called on to settle things between
your boys when you really have no idea who did what to
whom, who started it. Then, not blaming either of them, but
focusing on the act itself can let nature take its course: the
guilty party, or the more guilty one, will feel it and you
haven't had to do anything, especially make a mistake; you
haven't punished one who now feels resentful about his
brother getting off free—or punished both and left both
feeling treated unfairly.

"It's pretty easy to know what to do when one of them is
obviously the culprit. It's also fairly easy if both are equally at
fault. But when you really don't know, there's no need to
make a mistake. You don't have to be Sherlock Holmes to
realize that a scream is only circumstantial evidence. It really
doesn't tell you much—maybe just who can hit the hardest.
Nobody in the family has the right to break something belonging to someone else or hurt anybody and get away with it.
But if you arrive in the middle of a fight, you should keep in
mind that you're probably only seeing ten percent of the
scenario."

Here's an example that happened soon afterward.

By the Sea, By the Sea, By the Beautiful Sea

On a beautiful summer day Mother drove to the beach
with Mark and Peter. She was finally reading that novel
and getting a good tan. The boys were digging a big hole
to the People's Republic of China. After an hour or so,
she went back to the car to get their lunch and the cold
drinks. When she got back to the beach, the boys weren't

playing. Mark was throwing sand at Peter who was screaming bloody murder. Mark shouted, "He threw sand at me first!" Mother: "There is to be *no* throwing sand. That's rule number one when we come to the beach. I'm sorry I didn't get here sooner to see what happened. It's too late to go into that now. Let's take a quick swim to cool off and have some lunch."

Mother was away when Mark got tired of digging the hole. He decided to build a castle with roads around it for his toy cars. Peter wanted to join him but Mark said no, he wanted to do it himself. He knew digging a big hole together was fine because Peter could help with that. With something more important like a castle, a collaboration would be a mess because Peter, two years younger, was all thumbs. Peter was incensed at being excluded, stamped on the beginning of the castle, and kicked sand in Mark's face. Mark pushed him down and threw sand at him and just then Mother arrived.

It would have been easy for her to identify Mark as the culprit and punish him. But Peter had his part in it. When she was out of earshot, she lost touch with the chain of events. So she simply focused on the act of throwing sand. And she was wise enough not to try to get them to eat lunch quietly together right after such a row. They were still too excited. A transition period, a quick dip in the water, was needed.

Doesn't this violate the principle of making everyone responsible for their behavior, keeping the act attached to the person? Yes, and she might have dealt with it differently if she'd have been watching it develop, for Mark was asking for a fight by making Peter feel incompetent. Guilt assignment became very complicated. Why *not* deal with just the part she saw?

Let's say you're driving on the freeway and want to get home before dark. You speed up to a little over sixty. The speed limit is fifty-five. Still, cars keep passing you, going sixty-five and seventy. You're stopped by a policeman. As he's writing out the ticket, you say, "What about that car that just passed me doing seventy?" He says, "You were easier to catch." How would you feel?

Your children will actually feel safer with a ceiling on their impulses. So do set limits. No breaking of things that belong to anybody else. No hurting anyone. No stream of swearing and verbal abuse. There's no cookbook or formula; every family is different and has its own special circumstances and situations. There's no reason to let children "fight it out" or "settle it themselves" when they aren't able to. Don't ignore it and be party to an undeclared war in your household.

Face it: no matter what parents feel about the subject, disciplinary intervention is unavoidable in one form or another. Children have to learn to share, to wait, to respect others' rights, to learn to accept responsibility for their own behavior. The limits you set will unquestionably cause frustration and resentment since they'll see all rules as restrictive. Still, they need these limits if they're to learn to gain self-control and balance their own wishes against each other's. You'll make mistakes. Mistakes are inevitable and no permanent harm will occur if you genuinely love your children.

There are no perfect blueprints because there are such enormous variations in family values and because parents and children are all different in temperament. I have been impressed with the wide variety of ingenious ways parents have invented for coping with sibling rivalry. A wide range of techniques are effective. For example, some families control fighting by deliberately taking a uniform stand over and over. Whenever there is fighting between a brother and sister, *both* are held at fault. The elder is blamed for not giving in to the younger, and the younger is scolded for not respecting the elder. No matter what the cause of the fight, both are equally guilty. In these families, the emphasis is on learning a mutual respect for one another based on seniority and juniority. It suppresses fighting and both kids begin to check their own impulses. They learn that they can't manipulate and play innocent, that they're in it together and need to stick together.

Eventually that directs them toward their own problem-solving experiments. It eliminates the satisfaction one child gets from the punishment of another and does away with the idea that there's always one guilty and one innocent party, one good and one bad. It suggests that there's good and bad in everyone and that this is managed by developing a framework for brothers and sisters to see each other, according to age, each with responsibility for the other.

These general principles hold: take a stand. Don't be a faceless parent whose permissiveness is interpreted as lack of concern when children are fighting and would like to stop. Be someone they can predict. Draw a line and exert reasonable authority.

Parental Problems with Discipline

Let's see how things go wrong. The major errors in dealing with sibling rivalry are: (1) too much too soon, (2) too little too late, (3) inconsistency, and (4) disunity. My examples are extravagant because extremes may show you best how to identify problems in your family when they fall into these four patterns. Let's take a look at the first two families. I've named them the Hawks and the Doves.

Too Much Too Soon—The Hawks

It was Saturday. Mrs. Hawk said to her husband, "It's such a nice day. Why don't you take the children to the zoo?" He answered, "I will not! If the zoo wants them, let it come and get them!" Father was deathly afraid that the children, Nancy and Gerald, would fight in public. So they rarely went out. Much of this began one evening when the children were toddlers. Mr. Hawk came home and found his wife in tears. She said, "Gerald and Nancy have changed into monsters. Remember how they used to be so sweet when they were babies? Now they hit each other all the time! What'll we do?"

Mr. Hawk decided to train the kids along the lines of his own "Victorian" upbringing. They would sit at the table during meals and speak only when spoken to. He kept a paddle downstairs and another upstairs so he could spank them whenever it looked as if they were going to quarrel. (And regular paddling every evening was given them as a reminder to "be good.") Under this pressure, Nancy grew up to become chronically rebellious and vengeful, Gerald quiet and constricted, showing little or no emotional expression, a perfect little "gentleman." He was terrified of his father. Nancy, on the other hand, became totally immune to punishment. She attacked Gerald and said to her father, "Hit me some more, you can't hurt me!"

Mr. Hawk saw his children as a real threat to his authority and determined to stamp it out. He thought to himself, *They may not be strong enough now, but . . .* Their present weapons may look primitive, but given a couple of years they might develop atomic missiles! So he developed a policy of deterrence, a first-strike or preventive-action policy (constant warnings and daily spankings). He didn't see their behavior as immature and temporary; it would overwhelm him if not nipped in the bud.

When his young children began to fight with each other, he was frightened; to him, this signaled permanent personality changes. He took massive action, not realizing that restrictions were indeed needed but imposed gradually and firmly at the level the youngsters could handle. They needed help while their own controls were forming and they began to get to know each other.

Father's excessively punitive attitudes forced them into one of two alternative patterns: either chronic rebelliousness, open or indirect (to get revenge), or conformity and pseudo-maturity which produce the "too good child" with an enormously constricted personality and a narrowing of future potential. His children, unless he relaxes his expectations and standards, will end up as perfect little ladies and gentlemen or the other extreme—totally immune to severe punishment because it has been used indiscriminately.

Too Little Too Late—The Doves

Clint, seven, wearing his cowboy suit and boots, had a large chip on his shoulder. He was looking for a fight. His sister Elsie, nine, was talking to her friend on the telephone. He listened on the extension, made sounds into the receiver—beeps, clicks, squeals, and whistles. Elsie shouted, "Get off the phone!" He said, "I have just as much right as you do. Stick 'em up!" She made a face at him. He shot her with a cork from his toy pistol. She grabbed it and hit him over the head.

Mother heard them from the other room and rushed in with her bag of lollipops, giving two to each. Clint said, "I want another." She let him take another. He licked it and stuck it in his sister's hair. She screamed and kicked him in the shin. Mother said, "Please, children, why don't you do something quiet? Play a nice game together. Maybe your father will take us to the movie this evening if you're good." Clint shouted, "I want to go to the movie anyway," and Elsie agreed. They made their mother promise.

Mrs. Dove doesn't even try to deal with the normally powerful impulses of young Clint to control others. He is becoming a spoiled child because she uses the lollipop school of training to raise her children. The lollipoppers aren't even respectable leftovers from the "permissive era" of child rearing: Mrs. Dove doesn't even use the rewards for good behavior to reinforce it. Amazingly (but not uncommonly) she actually rewards obnoxious behavior!

The children test and probe her and find no limits. They never learn a reasonable accommodation to authority and will have trouble coping with everyday frustrations all their lives. They'll be unlikely to assume responsibility for their behavior because few demands are made on them to be just plain civilized and reasonably accommodating to others. Surprisingly, Clint and Elsie might develop the same kind of personality traits as Nancy and Gerald Hawk, the youngsters who were overdisciplined. They could either remain chronically immature—rebellious and antagonistic because their impulses are given free rein, or they could attempt to overcorrect themselves because they become frightened of what they do. This could make them overly inhibited and shy.

Mother doesn't set limits because she is afraid the kids will get angry with her. She's afraid of driving them away. The best she can do is a very general plea: "Please play quietly." Her rules are "soft" and meant to be broken. She needs to get quite specific and firm, clear about her directions, and guide them into other activities.

You can usually sense when your youngster is on the muscle and you can defuse it. If she had hooked in on Cowboy Clint with the Chip on His Shoulder, she might have decided to circle the wagons. "Okay, pardner, time to check your guns at the door, just like they do in the old western saloons! And then come into the kitchen and have some red-eye!" That friendly warning might have worked.

Warnings don't always do the trick. (We know traffic signs are important but they're often not enough to stop traffic violations.) If you give ample warnings and reminders first ("I'll give you until the count of three to get off the phone, Clint—your sister is talking on it") and they don't work, then you'll have to act as a policeman and give out a ticket, "Okay,

Clint Eastwood, the horse stays in the corral this afternoon—
no bike riding till tomorrow!"

The Waffles

The Waffle family had tried everything. Beth and
Mary, the two daughters, shared a room and resented it.
They were constantly into each other's clothes and toys,
fighing over whose things needed picking up, whose
turn it was for the bathroom. One morning before school,
Beth came screaming to her mother, "I was brushing my
teeth and she tried to push me aside. She won't let me
brush my teeth before school, Mother. What do you
think of that?" Mother answered, "Okay, both of you
lose your allowance this week for fighting." She'd let it
pass every morning so far but now suddenly decided to
take a stand. And what a stand! The two girls began to
cry. As they left for school, their mother apologized. "I
was really wrong in coming down so hard on you. I'm
sorry. No hard feelings?"

The girls found it easy to produce guilt in their mother. It's
because she saw discipline as a hostile act, something to feel
guilty about. So she tried to undo the guilt by alternating
permissiveness with strictness. She couldn't say yes or no or
follow through on a restriction, regulation, or expectation. She
tried everything but settled on nothing; she threatened but
didn't impose her standard. There was no consistent dealing
with the girls' behavior. If she could only realize what the
girls were doing to her and to each other, she could monitor
the bathroom use and have reasonable penalties for violations.
They needn't be so sudden an overreaction as taking away a
week's allowance. Perhaps that's why she apologized, indicating
she was wrong. Mrs. Waffle could have threatened the kids
with death row and the electric chair and they wouldn't have

blinked an eye. The sentence was far away, there would be plenty of time for appeal, and they knew she wouldn't have the heart to do it anyway.

The Crossfires

The Crossfires had company for dinner. Suddenly the three boys ran through the dining room shooting each other with water pistols. Racing through the hallway, they turned over a table and broke the lamp. The mock fight soon became real. Each blamed the other for the lamp disaster. After they had quieted down, Mother said it was bedtime. Father said, "Aw, let 'em stay up a little longer, it's a special occasion." Again, the kids made a scene. "Why do I have to go to bed earlier than he does?" "How come Tommy gets away with everything and I don't?"

Father laughed uncomfortably and said to his guests, "Well, I guess boys will be boys. Isn't it funny the way they fight?" Mother was exasperated and put all three of them to bed with their clothes on and told them there would be no television for a week. The boys giggled to each other in the dark. "She's so strict and Daddy's so easy. Let's stay away from her." "Maybe we can get him to take us to the baseball game tomorrow." "Yeah, especially if we promise him no fighting at the game." "Let's get up and pretend we're sleepwalking if we're caught."

Mr. and Mrs. Crossfire disagreed about discipline and couldn't find a common ground for working together or supporting each other in seeing a decision through. If you asked them, they would say they might not always agree on the approach to the youngsters' fighting, but their own attitudes toward each other were more important. Fine. Yet, the youngsters sensed that they really had no genuine respect for each other so they continued to run wild. The boys knew that when there were disagreements between the parents, they could manipulate them and play one against the other.

If the Crossfires had a united approach, they could handle the boys' acting up in front of company just by deciding, "You guys either will have to learn to stay in the other room and play quietly and go to bed on time when we have people over, or we'll get a baby-sitter. We'll try it one more time, but if you make another fuss at bedtime, from then on the baby-sitter will be here to handle it. And you won't be able to come down to see the company." But the boys knew they could appeal to their father and get the television restriction rescinded. A week was much too long anyway.

Avoid the four major errors in discipline, or correct them if you've seen yourself in the families described so far.

Now let's start developing an effective way to deal with fighting and a live and let live philosophy. Let's consider some methods and how to apply them flexibly.

Forms of Discipline to Use for Fighting

Children can learn best if it's not a parent's bias that determines punishment, but rather if the punishment is natural and follows as a logical consequence of behavior. It's simplest to remove whatever they're fighting over.

A Trojan Horse for Little Brother

Ned, three, was given his older brother's dump truck. Mark, six, had outgrown it. But one rainy weekend while Mark was watching "The Flintstones," his favorite TV show, he spotted Ned on the floor having a grand time with the truck. The Flintstones didn't matter anymore. All the fun that he used to have with that truck came back to him. "Here, Ned, let me help you work it." "No!" said

Ned loudly. "Come on, you little turkey, it's mine anyway," said Mark and grabbed the truck. But Ned was strong for his age. A tug-of-war brought Mother on the run.

It was the third time that day and she felt like a tire after the Indianapolis 500. She counted to ten (for her own sake) and said, "Okay, if you guys are going to fight over it, I'll have to take it away. It isn't really fair to Ned, because, Mark, you told us you were ready to give it up. There must be a little part of you inside that isn't ready yet. But I don't like the way you've been treating your brother today. If he's going to have to give up his dump truck I'm turning off your television show."

Mother had harnessed the basic essentials of discipline. She applied disapproval along with understanding, as well as simple deprivation (taking away the toy they were fighting over). If it *clearly* belongs to one child, it should naturally be his private property and the fight resolved in his favor. If lines of possession are blurred (in this case the truck recently belonged to Mark) it's probably best to put it away for the time being. Mother put it on the top shelf in her closet and helped Ned find some of his old toys. Mark busied himself with a puzzle.

The next day, when Mark was back in school, she brought the truck out and let Ned play with it in his room. He had fun with it there and kept it in his toy chest. Mark seemed to forget about it and the situation was resolved. The problem was not. They couldn't afford to buy new toys for Ned all the time. He'd just have to have some of Mark's as Mark went on to others. Perhaps a smoother transition could be found. It was.

When Mark graduated to a larger two-wheeled bicycle, his old one was ready for Ned to have with training wheels. Before turning it over to Ned, Father painted it a different color. Everyone knew whose bike it had been, but the new color seemed to make a difference. Mark was able to give it up. At the same time he was enjoying his larger bike and feeling more grown-up. He even helped Ned learn to ride without "accidentally" letting go of him once! Mother poured on the approval and Mark beamed: "Mark, you really are learning to let Ned have some of your old things and not be jealous. I know it's hard, and I really appreciate what you're doing, helping him to learn how to ride a two-wheeler like you can do."

Having used disapproval and simple deprivation (removal of the immediate source of the problem), the parents found ways in which they could improve things even more. They found the old car thief's trick of quickly repainting a car to change its former identity. And they combined this with a new bike for Mark. Finally, they praised him on his more mature behavior which was likely to lead to further sharing.

Approval and praise for periods of getting along and solving problems is primary. Next comes the use of disapproval, and of course the logical or natural consequences of behavior, removal of the source of fighting. Still, as all parents know, you can soon feel like a basketball referee after a particularly difficult game—running up and down the court, assessing penalties, taking the ball away for fighting, awarding foul shots—and this really doesn't get at the root of the problem. Further measures are necessary.

While some parents may be able to help their children develop self-control by using just disapproval (a temporary loss of affection), most need additional discipline. This involves punishment—an effort to produce an unpleasant experience for a reason. Its only justification is to produce a change in behavior. It's a remarkably complex contract between parent and children. To be effective at all, it must be "embedded in the family bosom": it only works in a loving atmosphere, a family where basic affection prevails most of the time. Punishment should never be motivated by revenge or sheer meanness.

No parent can raise children without an occasional loss of temper over their fighting. Mistakes are only human. But when you've lost your temper, you're punishing for *your* sake, not theirs. Your judgment is off-key. Your children have to be in just the right state to take punishment and have it work. Otherwise, no lesson will be learned. You need to make sure that the child can make use of the experience. The real test is how he or she reacts to the punishment, not whether you feel better or not.

Some parents are locked into one way of dealing with fighting. It reflects their personal preferences, not necessarily the youngsters' needs. For example, some parents won't use isolation, sending a youngster to his room, because they think it's cruel. They may spank instead! Others avoid corporal punishment at all costs (probably 80 percent or more use it sometimes). The important point is to throw a "mixed package" of the three major forms at the problem after disapproval is used up: (1) isolation; (2) deprivation of privileges, and possibly (3) physical or corporal punishment.

To Spank or Not to Spank?

Marge and Fred Thomas enjoyed the family dinner hour more than did their two young boys, Henry and Jimmy. Henry was slinging peas at Jimmy. Jimmy giggled and flung a glob of mashed potatoes back under the table. The boys had been at each other since Fred had come home from work. Fred was exasperated and said, "If you boys can't eat in a civilized way with the rest of the family, you'll have to eat by yourselves." He was using logical consequences of their behavior: isolation from the rest of the family if they couldn't be sociable.

Henry went to the TV room and Jimmy to the kitchen, each with their plates. Unfortunately this isolation wasn't enough. Henry enjoyed not having to sit up at the table and have his manners on display so he liked eating by himself. This was certainly no lesson for him. Jimmy, meanwhile, kept up the fighting from the kitchen. He called Henry appetizing names such as "Doodoo Head."

Fred decided to escalate sanctions a notch and take firmer action. "I want you each to go to your room for fifteen minutes." Henry went, but he didn't need fifteen minutes to cool off. He just needed to be separated from his brother and he would have snapped back quickly. Fred liked to give sentences of five minutes, fifteen minutes, or half an hour, even though sometimes they were too short and sometimes too long. Sometimes the youngsters weren't ready to come out of their rooms after a five-minute station break so their fighting continued. Other times they didn't need a full fifteen minutes or half hour and simply sat in their rooms brooding. They had cooled off and settled down.

Now they were heating up for a new fight because they were mad and felt unfairly treated. Fred might have been better off not to use fixed time-out periods. Rather, when the youngster and parent both agreed he was ready to come out, he came out.

At any rate, Jimmy refused to go: "I won't! You can't make me!" "Okay, young man, for every minute you stay here and refuse to go to your room, you'll go to bed ten minutes earlier tonight." Jimmy waited for one minute so no one could accuse him of giving in too fast and went. On his way he muttered under his breath, "I hate you! You're the worst goddamn meanest person in the world! I wish you were dead."

Fred said that bedtime would be ten minutes earlier and told Jimmy he couldn't come out of his room until he apologized for talking that way. When Fred sat down at the table fuming, Marge said, "I think both those boys need a good spanking. They've been at each other all day and I'm fed up with them. I'm glad you're home to see some of this."

This uneasy armistice raises several issues about punishment. Isolation (sending to a room) is probably best left flexible, rather than imposed with a fixed time limit, as I've said, because you can't tell ahead of time how many minutes it will take a youngster to settle down. Leftover anger might flood him if he comes back too fast; he'll sulk in the room if he's left there too long. Sometimes it's even wise to say, "Go to your room and try to figure out how to stop the fighting. When you have a solution, come on down and we'll discuss it."

Fred found one of his sons more stubborn than the other. Henry actually enjoyed the separation from the family meal, which certainly doesn't teach him a lesson. It seems almost better that Jimmy was angry. That meant he was ready for a lesson, in contrast to Henry, who was happy to eat by himself. But Jimmy's anger and stubbornness couldn't be ignored beyond a certain point. Fred couldn't just stand by and let him refuse to go to his room. So Fred shifted to an appropriate alternative, deprivation of privileges. He chose bedtime privilege and it worked.

Deprivation of privileges is most often effective, as in this case, if there has been a *continuation* of fighting or a problem which can't be dealt with by disapproval or simple isolation. Short restrictions of television, bike riding, playing outside, and allowances are common deprivations. On the way to his room, Jimmy needed to fire off a parting shot. Fred demanded an apology. He didn't lose his temper and spank him. He realized it was okay for Jimmy to be angry with him. In fact, the bedtime deprivation seemed to wake him up. He probably went to his room angry at his father but beginning to shift toward being mad at himself. If this happened, it would be just what was needed: a motivation to change—as long as he was not *too* angry and was angry at the right person, himself. If he slips into an orgy of self-pity or hatred of his parents, the effectiveness would be lost. It's what seeps down into his later behavior that counts.

So try not to produce *too* much panic or anger with your punishment—just enough to be effective. Also you had better realize that *many* small experiences with discipline, not just one great big one, are needed to make an impression on Henry and Jimmy. And the discipline must be administered not out of moral indignation but out of judgment of whether the youngster can make use of it or not.

Fred's requiring Jimmy to say he was sorry was really an attempt to help the youngster recover. A gesture, such as saying "I'm sorry," not only makes him feel comfortable with himself once he's cooled off; more important, it'll make it possible for Fred to like him again. This is the important issue—Fred has to be able to forgive him. "Say you're sorry" is often overused by parents. Also, "I'm sorry" can be used by a youngster as a manipulation, a fake conciliatory gesture to buy himself back into parental good graces. If not overdone, it's a legitimate ounce of flesh he gives to clear the air.

What about Marge's feelings that "they each need a good spanking"? She had been with the boys all day. They'd been picking at each other over every little thing. Marge raises the most controversial form of punishment—spanking. Physical punishment isn't in itself harmful as long as the bottom line for children is that they feel wanted. That's more important than whether they get spanked or not. You usually can't tell from observing a family whether spanking is used or not because some families use spanking and love their children very much. Then there are families who would never use it but who reject them—and constant humiliation is worse. Continual humiliation is much more damaging than an occasional spanking.

Jimmy Carter's younger sister, Gloria, recalls that switching with a light peach tree branch was preferred when they were growing up because it was over with fast. "It wasn't a bad switching. It was just to let us know not to do it again. And we didn't. The worst punishment that could happen to us would be for Daddy to go out on the front porch and call one of us by our name. My Daddy never called us by our name unless it was something very serious and that meant he was going to ask us about something that we knew we had done already, and he was going to give us a lecture. Oh, that was horrible."*

Spanking is perhaps the form of punishment most often misused by parents, so caution is needed before you spank. It should be limited and controlled, and restricted to younger children, for whom a slap on the "offending part," that is, the hand or the foot that "did the fighting," will fit into the younger child's way of thinking. It should be limited to a quick slap on the hand or buttocks, never on the face. And it may clear the air of prolonged nagging that hangs over the household like smog and more quickly restore a normal relationship between parent and child.

Spanking (or physical punishment generally) should never be the main form of discipline. It should be the last resort, not the first choice. It's mainly to make the child *remember*. It should never be used by a parent during loss of temper. Then it'll be interpreted by the child as an assault. The parent who uses it more for his or her own benefit than for the child's is likely to feel remorseful and guilty when the realization dawns.

Physical punishment, if administered at all, should be given at the time the offense is committed in order to cut it short, especially one that's being repeated over and over again, e.g., fighting between Jimmy and Henry. It should never be stored up and dished out later when the child can't remember what it's for. Nor should it exceed one or two slaps. If a parent employs physical punishment at all, personal responsibility should be taken for it: use your own hand, not weapons or instruments, the traditional hairbrush, strap, paddle, or belt. If Marge had seen the boys slugging it out during the afternoon, she might have swatted each on the seat of the pants or added a slap on the hand for emphasis.

You may be surprised that I condone physical punishment at all. And give a description of how to do it! I can almost

* De Mause and Ebel, *Jimmy Carter and American Fantasy.*

hear you asking: What kind of child psychiatrist is this? Once again, this is certainly not the best (and probably the most overused) form of discipline. But the fact that it seems to be considered necessary by the majority of parents makes me feel there should be an open discussion of its use. Just labeling it harmful and dangerous hardly faces the reality that it always has been used and always will be, no matter what I say.

If physical punishment is needed with younger children, it should diminish and disappear as they grow older. The important point to remember is that punishment is only justified when it teaches children something *in addition* to stopping behavior. That's why punishing children for fighting when they're in the midst of a joint temper tantrum is useless. Timing is important. And it's important to get it over as quickly as possible. Avoid prolonged shame or moralizing reminders that keep problems, blames, and hurts alive. Try to find a way to clear the slate. Don't grudgingly withhold forgiveness longer than necessary.

In our present case, Fred went to Jimmy's room after a few minutes and sat down on the bed. Jimmy said, "I'm sorry, Dad." "That's okay, Jimmy. I think I know how you felt when you said you hated me. When you said you wished I was dead, you really meant you were very mad at me and wished I was out of your way. I guess there's no one who doesn't get that mad sometimes and wish people out of the way, including me. We don't have to love each other every single minute, just most of the time. But I won't have you swearing at me. That has to stop in this house.

"It's okay to feel angry at us sometimes; and, heaven knows, you and Henry are mad at each other a lot! What you *do* about it is another thing entirely. You and Henry will slowly learn how to argue with each other better. Then you won't have to show it by throwing things or hitting each other as much. And Mom won't want to give you a swat when she's fed up to here."

Discussion of the feelings behind misbehavior is the goal. If discipline leads to that end and isn't an end in itself, it suggests that children are maturing. It also means the parents are mature and want them to grow up to a higher level of dealing with problems between people.

Jimmy replied, "You know, Dad, it all started this morning when I was doing my darn piano practice before school and it wasn't going right. You know how much Mom wants me to play the piano and how much I hate it. So I was sitting there thinking about how mad I was at her and I was swearing at the piano. Just then, Henry came by and smiled! That got it going. I guess I was really mad at Mom about the piano, but it's hard to blow up at her. It's easier for Henry and me to fight. Then I finally exploded at you tonight. Sometimes I just don't know who I'm mad at."

Fred: "Well, pal, I think we're getting somewhere, because that's often the way it really is; sometimes we don't really know what or whom we're mad at. Sometimes it's even ourselves we're really mad at."

Jimmy said, "Good night, Dad. I guess it's time for me to go to the penalty box for that ten minute early bedtime. Might as well get it out of the way. Right?"

Marge and Fred talked more about it when the boys had gone to bed. Mother was in favor of banishment to the bathroom rather than the youngsters' bedroom because there were toys in the bedroom with which they could have fun when they were supposed to be punished. Father disagreed. He felt that the point was to remove them from the company of the rest of the family, and having a child sit in a corner looking at the wall was just too humiliating. Mother felt that the length of time, which was so important to Father, was less important than the way you applied it. She felt it was very hard to set just the right sentence for a particular crime. Should it be five minutes for ripping your own book and ten minutes for ripping a library book? She did have some success telling the boys that they could come out when they stopped crying or screaming for a few minutes. Then she would explain to them why they were sent to their room; now she had their attention about their bad behavior.

Marge said, "I guess the main thing is for us to be consistent and use isolation first, taking away privileges second, and spanking last. Sometimes I get too fed up. If there was a gun handy, I would shoot them. That's when I'm most likely to lose my temper and spank them, and it doesn't make sense."

Fred: "Well, we all lose our tempers sometimes. I guess almost every parent has felt like killing the kids sometime or other. The difference is in who has the brakes to control themselves and who doesn't. And often we don't even know who we're mad at. I was just talking to Jimmy and he told me he didn't know who he was really mad at today when he was getting in fights with people. I guess it's like me and my problems at the office, when I come home and take it out on you and the kids."

Marge: "The hardest thing for me is sticking with what works best. Separating them when they're fighting and sending them to their rooms works fine at home. But when I'm visiting at Ann's house and have them with me, and they start fighting there, oh, brother! It's even worse at the supermarket. I warn them when they're running up and down the aisles chasing each other and maybe knocking over somebody's cart full of groceries. But they don't even listen to me!"

Fred: "I guess maybe that's when you have to bite the bullet and just go home right then. Could you interrupt your shopping and go home so you can carry out your warning—putting them in their rooms?"

Marge: "I guess so. I haven't tried that because I don't have the time to waste. But I'd probably only have to do it once. It'd ruin my shopping for one day, but they'd learn the lesson. I guess I could also dock their allowance if they misbehave in public."

Fred: "Yeah, I've tried that, too. But I've been burned. Sometimes they don't remember why I'm taking it out of their allowance the week after it happened. That makes me feel extra bad because they obviously didn't learn any lesson. They're just mad and feel put down."

Marge: "Yes, you've got to be specific and right on top of things. When I tell them clearly what I expect of them and state the consequences, it seems to work better too, especially if I reexplain it later when the consequences have happened! And when I tell them *why* I'm praising them, it's much better than just praising them and saying, 'You sure are good boys.' The main thing I've found is that sometimes I've only been responding to negative behavior like fighting. I ignore the positive stuff when they get along, as if I take it for granted. It's kind of like giving Henry and Jimmy brownie points for the time they don't fight but no brownie points for the time they play well together."

How Behavior Modification Works

At the PTA meeting the other night, the guest speaker was talking about behavior modification, a way for parents to work with their kids over fighting by using rewards and punishments in the right amounts.

Fred: "Yeah, I got the feeling that setting up those systems is like setting up a cashier's window. You pay out or take in points, and you're more involved in the points than in the kids and what's going on between them."

Marge: "Not necessarily. You can make privileges such as special TV watching and special activities contingent on earning points doing chores together. Or if they go all day Saturday without a major fight and are obviously settling things better themselves, they can get to go to a movie on Sunday as an extra treat because they put in extra effort. It's better to keep track one day at a time than saying, 'Don't fight at all.' And it makes them pay more attention to how they are getting along. It makes them think about their fights."

Fred: "Yes, I remember that speaker talking about setting up a point system. You get points for doing things together, playing or doing chores, and you lose them for fighting. At the end of the day the points are exchanged for their daily allowance or saved for something special. But it seemed to me that the end of the day wasn't just for exchanging points and totaling them up. It was a time when the parents and kids could meet and discuss what had gone on during the day."

Marge: "Right. The points themselves don't have any real worth. They're valuable because they can be exchanged for privileges and they give the kids positive feedback about their behavior. It gives them *and* us a new way and a fresh start when the old ones aren't working. And it's a clear-cut way to take us out of the arguing and nagging that goes on all day between them. You're not here so you don't know what it's like. And with the point system you can always be flexible. You can lower or raise what the kids need to get special privileges. I'd kind of like to try it. The fighting and calling each other names, breaking toys and sometimes my furniture—that's really the biggest problem I have with them. I could send them to their rooms as the main punishment and a loss of ten points if they won't go. If they play well together for ten minutes they should *get* as many points as they'd have been losing. I'd make it ten minutes because I've never seen them play longer than that."

Fred: "Well, maybe we should start with five minutes if you really want to try it. But what do we use for rewards?"

Marge: "Maybe we should start by splitting their weekly allowance up into daily amounts. But then we could set up special rewards, too, like an extra hour before bedtime in the evening and special desserts they like. It might just get them to work together to get these things rather than fight all the time over which one thinks he's my favorite. They might get the point if they have to work for those treats *together*."

Fred: "But how would you tell whether they played together well for ten minutes unless you watched? Have you got all day? You might even have to sit and watch their game and give points when one waits and takes his turn or tells the other that it's his turn or sticks to a rule or doesn't get upset when he's losing."

Marge: "I wouldn't mind doing that. It might even be fun as an experiment."

Fred: "Well, maybe. Let's try it and see if it works. If it works and things get quieter for a few weeks, we can begin to phase it out. I wouldn't want us to lean on it forever. I'm really more interested in seeing them learn how to communicate better and to negotiate with each other."

Encouraging Kids to Communicate

Discipline or specific behavioral approaches aren't the whole answer. They may change things on the surface, the way things look, the way youngsters act toward each other. But behavior is determined by the way you feel inside, too. This is the stuff that sibling rivalry is made of—anger, jealousy, envy, loneliness. Youngsters need to understand what these feelings are, what generates them and how to manage them.

There *are* ways to undo these negative but normal feelings. One is to develop empathy, an understanding of how the other person feels, putting yourself in the other person's shoes.

Sometimes we assume that understanding the way we and others feel is acquired naturally as we grow up. Actually, it can be taught—or remain totally undeveloped if you neglect it. Learning to understand one's own needs and feelings requires a continual round of talking about them, first between the parents and children, then between the kids themselves. These days, this essential process of communication among family members has been drastically changed—sometimes even replaced—by television. To compound the problem, television can make sibling rivalry worse, as every parent knows. What to do?

I Never Saw a Purple Cow, I Never Hope to See One

Ken, nine, was watching "The Six Million Dollar Man," his favorite program. His younger sister and brother, Katie and John, six and four, had to watch what Ken had turned on. But they couldn't understand the story. Suddenly, out of nowhere, John threw a toy car at Katie, missing her and hitting the TV set. He yelled, "I want to watch Superman!"

Ken said, "It's not on now, you dummy!" and turned up the volume. "If you don't want to watch this, get out of here. Now shut up."

Katie said, "We will not." Ken reached out and knocked their heads together. Katie and John screamed. Mother stopped what she was doing and came in: "What's going on in here?" She saw the toy automobile lying on the floor under the chipped TV cabinet.

"Okay, this is the second time tonight. Off with the TV!"

Ken said, "No! It's the middle of my favorite program!"

Mother ordered: "Each of you go to your room! We'll talk afterward when everybody has settled down."

Later, when they were in the kitchen having their bedtime snack, she asked them what had happened, trying to trace the story back from the time she came in: "What made Katie and John scream, Ken?"

Ken answered, "Because I knocked their heads together with my bionic arm to keep them quiet. They were making too much noise and John threw something at the TV set."

"Ken, do you really think you have a bionic arm?"

Ken answered sheepishly, "Well, sometimes I do when I'm watching the show and imagine myself in it, but I know I really don't when the show isn't on."

Mother: "John, why did you throw the car?"

John: "Because Ken was mean to me and I saw the man on TV throw a car."

Mother: "Look, kids, seems to me this program helps to start fights between you. John, you and Ken seem to think that what you see on TV is real and you even imitate it. Why did the man throw the car?"

John: "I don't know."

Mother: "That's the trouble, you just saw something he did and then did it yourself without knowing why he did it in the story. And, Ken, even though you're older, I guess you're not old enough yet to keep the program you're watching separate from the way you deal with your brother and sister, even though you know we have a rule in the house that nobody is to hit anyone."

Ken: "But he deserved it."

Mother: "It sounds as if you've gotten the idea from TV programs that violence is okay, no, maybe the only or *best* way, as long as it's on the side of the law. That just isn't so. There are plenty of other ways to solve problems that they don't show on the TV programs you watch because the show has to get it over with. So shoot them. It saves all the time and trouble of arresting them and bringing them to court."

"What's court?"

"Well, it's a place where you talk things over to decide what's right and if someone should get punished for doing wrong. In a way, we're doing that now. John, you and Katie could have gone into the other room and found something else to do if you didn't want to watch Ken's show. Ken, you could have asked me to help or brought them to the kitchen if you'd been willing to give up a minute or two of your show."

Ken: "But you don't just sit around and talk about things and give up your show for a couple of brats."

Mother: "I guess that's what comes across on television—that it's a sign of weakness to talk and work things out. On TV there're only good guys or bad guys. Somebody's always supposed to be wrong; *doing* something is the only way to solve problems. That's how very *little* children look at the world. Now, John, you didn't know why the man on TV threw a car at people; you threw one anyway because you saw it happen. You know, those programs are only thirty or sixty minutes long, so things are solved in a hurry. That's not how things really happen in life. Problems go on and on. Like between you guys!"

Later that night a worried mother talked to her husband: "I think we better figure out which shows they can watch. I used to think it was all harmless and watching violence on TV was just a way to blow off steam. But now I'm convinced that sometimes TV actually stimulates fights between them. They think it shows how things really are, and they seem to be learning that violence is the only way to solve things. John and Katie are so young they don't even understand what leads up to a violent scene they watch on TV. The fighting just seems to be exciting for them."

Father: "Well, they say television is the third parent, the one that teaches them the most, because most kids in the country watch several hours a day. It sounds as if *we* need to teach them how we solve problems, sometimes arguing, working out alternatives and compromises, hopefully not by hitting each other."

Mother: "And I think it's about time to limit the TV watching. Ken always says the Hendersons and the Greens let their kids watch all they want, so we've gone along as if we have to be like them. Let's be different. After all, this is our family! If the kids get mad, okay. If they can't handle certain programs then they shouldn't watch. It's funny—we don't let them watch X-rated movies but we let them watch anything they want on TV even though a lot of their fighting goes on around it."

So the family set certain hours for TV watching and every Sunday they selected programs for the week from the *TV Guide*. The parents limited total TV time and also selected programs for content by watching some shows with the kids. They noticed what shows seemed to portray life situations much as in a real family and showed the ways of working things out that didn't rely simply on magic powers or violence, with everything and everybody labeled either good or bad. Mother noticed some other things that concerned her. For example, in westerns and detective serials, so many people are knocked unconscious so often that it becomes as routine as eating dinner. But they never show evidence of brain damage, even after weeks and weeks of blows to the head and spells of unconsciousness. What does that teach children about hitting each other? Probably that there is no harm in it.

One Saturday morning Mother was watching cartoons with John and Katie. They were absorbed in the action. Their favorite heroes, Superman, the Green Lantern, and Batman, were dealing with evil members of the Legion of Doom. Next came the animal cartoons. They seemed violent, though in a different way. The animals, a cat and a mouse, were chasing each other. The mouse was using reasoning and trickery to outwit the cat. The cat was thrown off a cliff, electrocuted, flattened, smashed, splattered. He always bounced back and got back in the fight again, only to lose at the end.

Mother could understand that they rooted for the "little guy," the underdog who outwitted the bigger and more powerful cat. But John lost interest in the cartoons. He shrouded himself with the linen tablecloth to resemble a cape and was running around the room. "I'm powerful, the most powerful on earth, and I fight for the oppressed!"

Katie said, "Stop that or I'll zap you!"

"Go ahead and try it! I dare you!" (John was an admirer of the ancient samurai warrior who provoked his opponent to attack first so he could learn the opponent's vulnerability and better plan a counterattack.)

Katie zapped him with a cushion.

"Aw, that didn't hurt," he said confidently. "Watch me disintegrate you."

At this point, Mother stepped in and turned off the set. The children were still "in shape" for discussion because she'd intervened early enough. The program was over anyway. She decided it was her job to protect them from each other and from the rather frightening identification with television characters. She wanted to explain what was real and what wasn't real and try to defuse the situation.

"What's all this good guy–bad guy stuff?"

John: "I've been sent to earth to punish evil!"

"John, I know you're just playing Captain Galaxy, but you go too far."

John: "With my cape, I look like him, so why shouldn't I act like him?"

Mother: "It's okay to play television games. I suppose at school if you hadn't watched them you wouldn't even know how to play them with the other kids, and you'd be left out. But you've got to know how and when to stop yourself and not bring Captain Galaxy into your problems with your sister just because you've watched him so much. Look, John, everybody has some good and bad in them. Even Captain Galaxy, if he were real, would have some faults and problems just like we all do. Katie, you zapped John just like you were trying to do what they do on TV cartoons."

Katie: "Sure, that's what happens to bad guys. I mean, guys who act bad sometimes."

Mother: "I noticed all those animals getting squashed, burned, and flattened, but they're always okay afterward. Is that the way it really is?"

Katie: "Of course not. That's the way it is on TV: it's make-believe."

Mother: "How would those guys feel if it *really* happened to them, like getting hit by a brick?"

Katie: "I guess they'd cry because it'd hurt."

John: "And they'd probably bleed and maybe even get knocked out."

Mother: "That's right! On TV all this violent stuff goes on without anybody getting hurt or having pain. But you remember when we had to take you to the hospital for stitches, John?"

John: "Yeah, it hurt a lot, and I was scared, too."

Mother had separated the children's fantasies from their real relationship with each other. She tried to help the kids establish boundaries and brakes they could use to move in and out of imaginary roles which are normal for children to play. She also gave them a lesson in empathy to make up for television's failure, particularly in cartoons, to show a victim's pain and injury, suffering and tears.

You're badly needed to help your children relate their own experiences to the artificial ones they see on television (and which they secretly wish for). If you do, they'll find a balance between real life and fantasy. Mother helped John reach the point of recognizing his own vulnerabilities and fears. She also pointed out one way they got angry at each other so that problems arise.

The solution wasn't discipline. She was lucky enough to be able to teach the kids a lesson because she'd watched the program with them. This enabled her to do more than intervene and settle things. She moved her children along on their way toward understanding and settling conflicts themselves. She moved them beyond TV's level, the notion that might makes right, force settles things and nobody is really hurt. This level may not undermine a preschool child's thinking, which already works that way, but it will set off major problems if children stay put there. And much of television works to keep them at that primitive level.

You'll discover other situations that give you openings for more than mere disciplinary intervention. Look for situations in real life that you can use to help youngsters themselves *think* about their problems with brothers and sisters, not just react from habit. Here's an example of how opportunities present themselves.

Brotherly Love Comes Later

Edward, seven, was always following around his older brother, Tim, ten. He tried to imitate him but was frustrated because the difference in age left him less skillful. The normal gap between their manual dexterity saw to it that Tim won all games. Edward would get furious and couldn't understand. He wouldn't accept a handicap because he thought he was just having bad luck. Or maybe there was something the matter with him and if he could overcome it he would be Tim's equal!

Jealousy mounted. It was particularly difficult because they were on the same Little League team. Tim rubbed it in, smiling when Edward struck out or dropped the ball. Tim was the captain of the team and Edward the youngest player. Tim: "You're never going to catch up. I'm bigger than you are." Edward: "Yes I am, you dick, just wait."

One day, they visited cousins who lived in the country. Their youngest cousin, Julie, four, followed them around everywhere. Finally, they went pleading to their parents, "Won't somebody get rid of her? She's spoiling everything! Why should we have to take care of her? We're out here to have fun and we want to ride the horses. She's too small and gets in the way. She's a pain in the neck!"

Mother and Father glanced at each other. They realized that a lecture—"Be nice to your little cousin, it's her farm—you're grown-up and should be responsible for her—you should love her and be willing to help her," etc.—would mean losing a golden opportunity. Instead they played dumb, listened as Edward went on and on about the injustice of his having to play with Julie because he was so much better and could do more things. They let Edward be the expert in describing the difference between ages and the discrepancy in skills because of it. Finally, when he'd finished, it took very little nudging to get him to see that his jealousy and fighting with Tim was exactly what he was criticizing in Julie. He smiled and said, "I guess that's why Tim wants to do things without me sometimes."

When You Discuss Sibling Rivalry Directly

There's nothing wrong with observing and reflecting back to brothers and sisters their problems of behavior: who starts what fights, situations that tend to generate them, how one sibling may or may not pick up a cue from the other and overreact to it. In sibling rivalry each reacts automatically to a good deal of subtle behavior. George smiles while his sister coughs up several thousand dollars in a game of Life. The smile is just enough to infuriate her and break up the game when she'd been holding herself together quite well over such a big loss and payoff.

Mother might say, "George, how do you think Linda felt when you rubbed it in? She was already feeling bad enough about losing," or "How would your friends at school react if you did that?" or "Do you really want the game to end this way?" If he doesn't, you could ask what he could do differently next time to get what he wants, a clean win. ("Let's switch positions, George—if she smiled when you were losing, what would you feel like doing?")

This direct discussion of behavior is threatening to most youngsters. They really don't want to examine their relationships. It has to be done very gently, delicately. It can be done indirectly in such a way that youngsters discover the patterns themselves, with a little help from you acting as a "midwife." If the parents had asked Edward to make a "New Year's resolution" ("I'll never fight with Tim again; I'll never be jealous of him because he's older and better at things than I am"), they would have destroyed the effectiveness of his eventually learning from his own experience. And besides, you know what happens to New Year's resolutions even among adults. "Next year I'm going to lose twenty-five pounds" or "Next year I'm going to stop smoking and start exercising" are vows notorious for their short life.

Still, you *can* look at (and discuss) sibling rivalry with your children. Often they're afraid if they examine the relationship they'll somehow come out on the short end or be branded as the guilty party or be forced to become the one who is supposed to change. That's why they hurl accusations back and forth at each other rather than discussing issues. Everybody knows that young children are much more inclined toward action than reasoning. But they also harbor the fear "If I talk to him about it, I'll lose," and they tend to act as if this is an automatic outcome. You need to convince them that they can really make *two* separate decisions: to talk about it and whether or not to do something about it.

The Sibling Diary

One way to discover patterns of sibling rivalry is to get a record (or log) to pinpoint them with your youngsters' help. Then you can zero in on specific problems *they've* identified rather than ones you point out, which may reflect your own bias and turn them off.

Rub-a-Dub-Dub, Two Kids and the Tub

Amy, eleven, and Mike, nine, were driving their parents crazy. The fighting went on all day long and seemed to carry over from one situation to another like chain lightning. Each child was like a porcupine ready to shoot out a quill at the other anytime. Unable to make sense out of this warfare and wanting to find something they could get a handle on, the parents asked the kids if they would each keep a "diary" about problems with each other for the next twenty-four hours. They agreed eagerly, because each felt this was a great opportunity to indict the other on paper and be the innocent victim.

At the end of twenty-four hours, the diaries were collected but not read. "Now just to make sure," said Father, "let's do it for another twenty-four hours." So they did. The next day, they all sat down and read the description of specific episodes in each diary. There was no question: fights flared up where they usually do between youngsters—in front of the television, at the table, in the kitchen. The diaries made clear that both children agreed most fights raged between 5:00 P.M. and bedtime. Narrowing it down further, it seemed clear that the fighting-est time was just before bedtime. Another peak period seemed to be in the morning before breakfast. And the most frequent and worst fights seemed to be about the bathroom they shared.

As Mother and Father compared the incidents in the two diaries, Amy and Mike began to respond to them.

Mike: "She spends a year in the bathroom."

Amy: "What could *he* be doing on the toilet for so long?"

Mike: "She uses too much hot water and there isn't any left."

Amy: "My hair is longer than yours so I need a longer shower."

Mike: "I'm always cleaning up her mess."

Mother interrupted. "Now at least we know what most of the fights are about. I guess sharing a bathroom isn't the easiest thing in the world." She also made a note to herself that the fight was being reenacted right in front of her, but she stayed relatively calm because it was a "laboratory-induced" fight; she was the scientist trying to analyze it. In this role, Mother found she could stay away from arguing, overriding, or denying their experience and feelings about a situation that seemed so explosive, the bathroom.

She said, "Now, I'd like the two of you to talk to each other for a few minutes about how we could make it easier on both of you. You know, like time schedules, alternating who goes first, one not always cleaning up, and the rest. Go ahead. Dad and I will help if you want us to."

Amy: "I'll pick up after myself if you don't take so long."

Mike: "I won't take so long if I can go first sometimes. I'm the youngest and I only get to be first once in a while, so I make up for it and take my time. The youngest shouldn't have to clean up all the time just for being the youngest so I'm glad you're volunteering. But you better keep your part of the bargain or I'll really get you!"

They begin to untangle the "why" of what is going on between them. As they resolve their differences and discover that they can actually negotiate, it's much like the way countries deal with each other. When two countries have border problems and the invader finds himself in too deep and decides to withdraw, the usual official communiqué starts loftily: "Our forces are withdrawing in the interests of peace. But if we are attacked, we will punish the aggressors severely." The other country also issues a face-saving communiqué: "Our government will allow the enemy forces to withdraw peacefully. But if there is any looting or provocation, they will be attacked and punished severely." Each backs off a bit with the necessary growling threats so as not to appear weak.

And yet, this is also the beginning of a solid agreement based on recognizing the rights of others as well as strength. Mother had found the solution or at least the means to a solution. Instead of screaming at the kids to stop fighting, she had them pinpoint and reenact a fight in slow motion so it could be dealt with dispassionately with hope for a solution at least. The one that came from them was likely to work longer than if it had been imposed.

The Instant Replay

You can also get youngsters to look at their relationships relatively painlessly (and set the stage for peace negotiations) with a small portable tape recorder. Children love to hear their own voices. If you record a fight between them and then play it back, they can "hear" themselves after the fact, when they've calmed down. Then they can listen and react with relative detachment. It's probably best to keep a tape recorder wherever most of the fighting rages, such as the room with the television set. Do get their general consent before you start this method. It's best as a springboard for discussion and as a beginning of resolving problems that aren't well understood.

Beneath the Golden Arch

Mother kept the tape recorder by the kitchen sink. The children, Charlie, Doug, and Sue, all knew it was there. In fact, they loved to use it themselves with Mother's supervision. Mother had just brought home a generous take-out order from McDonald's for Saturday lunch. Before the Big Macs were unwrapped, Charlie was eating French fries from Doug's carton.

Doug screamed, "You're eating my French fries, you dirty pig!"

Charlie: "They gave you more than they gave me! And McDonald's French fries are the best in the whole wide world! But they cheat! We've got to even it out."

Susie (eating her dessert first): "There aren't any cherries in this pie. I'll bet Doug and Charlie have 'em all!"

Fortunately, Mother had flipped the switch and it was all being recorded. Now she said: "Wait a minute. Hold it! Before you kids finish your lunch, I want you to hear this."

"Okay, Mom," was the chorus. She played it back and they began to laugh.

Doug: "Did I really say that? Boy, do I sound funny."

Charlie: "Is that the way I am?"

Mother: "Yes, it does seem silly when you hear it played back after it's all over, doesn't it? It's even funnier when you've cooled off and don't feel so mad and can listen to yourself. It's like listening to another person, isn't it? Well, maybe there are two people in everybody; like a big one, ten years old in you, Charlie, and a little two-year-old, too. The two-year-old was just talking on tape. Anyhow, kids, what're you going to do?"

Doug: "I think from now on we ought to count all the French fries first."

Charlie: "Naw, let's just take our chances."

Doug: "Okay, but if it happens too often, we'll have to trade."

The fighting had been contagious. Listening to her brothers, Susie had even begun to get a little paranoid about the cherries in her pie. Now they're beginning to negotiate. It's very tentative. At first, each is afraid of being vulnerable and "getting less" than the other, and that can't be tolerated with something as precious as McDonald's French fries.

Tallulah Bankhead would have sympathized with Charlie.

When she and her younger sister, Eugenia (Daddy's pet, according to Tallulah), picked blackberries together, Tallulah usually came home with more. After all, she was older and Eugenia was nearsighted. But when she didn't, Tallulah says she "ate from Eugenia's basket to equalize the yield."*

Remember the last time you went to buy a new car? You probably negotiated with the salesman about the price. You and he kept splitting the difference, with you starting from a very low and he from a very high one. He says he's your friend, but the manager won't budge another fifty dollars. He gets the manager to come down twenty-five dollars if it comes out of the salesman's (your friend's) commission. He likes you so much he'll do it just for you.

Finally you buy the car, feeling triumphant that you got the best possible discount from the sticker price. When the salesman says, "Boy, I'm glad I don't have to deal with you every day; you really know how to bargain," you literally glow! Still, on the way home you wonder, Did I really get the best of that or did he? How much farther would he have come down if I'd held out? Was he really playing a game he knew he would win?

Storytelling

You can't deal directly with this fear of "getting less." It strikes too sensitive a nerve. Anyone who is afraid of being weak and vulnerable, prey to being taken advantage of by such a natural predator as a brother or sister, must act superindependent and strike first, before it happens to him or her. There are ways to get this point across to children if you disguise it well enough. Read them children's stories that use the predator theme. Or why not make up stories? The hidden message will get through.

*Lee Israel, *Miss Tallulah Bankhead* (New York: G. P. Putnam's Sons, 1972).

Once Upon a Time

It's bedtime.

Doug: "Dad, tell me that story of the hunter again."

Dad: "Okay, pal. Once upon a time there was an old fellow named Joe who lived all by himself in a cave. He was surrounded by wild animals. He was afraid lots of the time because he lived alone in the middle of Indian territory. So he always kept a lot of fires going and made a lot of noise and shot his gun in the air every time he saw an Indian or a wild animal. That would scare them off. Trouble was, he never made any friends! And he hardly had any time to work in his garden or hunt for his food. He was just too worried all the time. He couldn't even sleep, it was getting so bad!" . . .

You can embellish the story, make it longer by adding twists and turns and an ending about the need for friendships and trust and that it isn't necessary to act powerful when you're afraid. It doesn't solve the problem.

In your story, maybe Joe finally talks to the Indians. Once he gets to know them and their lives, they work together as neighbors. Together, they keep the wild animals (common fears) away. Without ever lecturing to your child about the significance of the story, you can be pretty sure that the underlying message will penetrate, particularly if you tell several such stories with different characters and variations on the theme. Growl a lot and be enthusiastic as you play different parts. Children will ask for a story over and over again, mainly because it hits a personal chord. And it helps them find ways to get along better because it shows alternative solutions to fighting.

Role Playing

Another way to get children to distance themselves from their behavior and take a look at it (as well as put themselves in the shoes of a brother or sister) is role playing.

... And the Dog Jumped over the Moon

Cleopatra, the family basset hound, had puppies. Three were given away but the most active one, who loved to chase his own tail, was kept as the childrens' pet. Emily, ten, and Gardner, seven, had been told they would have to take care of the puppy if they wanted to have one. So, following their own logic, they divided up the dog into parts that they would each care for. Emily, the oldest, had the solution worked out:

"The front half of Fido (they named him Fido because they figured nobody else would think of that name) will belong to me and the back half to you, Gardner. That means I'll have to feed him all the time and you just take care of the other part."

Gardner: "No! I want the front part 'cause that's the part you pet and the part that you can teach to catch a ball."

Emily: "You don't know enough to train him. And he's going to have to sleep in my room besides."

Gardner stamps his foot and tries to grab Fido away from her. Emily hits him. Fido falls squirming to the floor and squeals. Mother arrives and says, "What's going on here?"

Gardner: "She hit me!"

Mother: "She wouldn't hit you without a reason."

Gardner: "Who ever said she needed a reason? You're always on her side! Why does she always get everything she wants?"

Mother realized she had made an error: "she wouldn't hit you without a reason" was taking sides and Gardner was saying so. And she hadn't really known what had gone on. Why pick on Gardner? He was beginning to feel he always got blamed. So she changed her tack and said: "You know, I think we ought to go over this whole argument again. But let's do it another way. Gardner, you be Emily and, Emily, you be Gardner." Both looked puzzled.

Emily said: "But how can I be him?"

Mother: "Just pretend."

Emily, sulking and trying to be Gardner, used a whining voice: "You get to name the dog because you're the oldest and a girl, and that's why Mommy lets you do things first."

Gardner, trying to be Emily, used a high-pitched, bossy, self-righteous voice: "I'm going to take the best part because I'm the oldest and give you the part that you have to clean up after."

Emily, in a pleading voice: "It's not fair. Let's own him equally, only not in parts. I'll feed him one week and you feed him the other, and we'll both train him to do doo-doo outside."

Mother: "See how easy it is for you to know what the other one is thinking and how it helps to get it out in the open? Emily, you even found the solution, by making yourself and Gardner into one person. Now you can work out something that's fair. Emily sometimes says she thinks Gardner is favored because he's youngest and Gardner thinks Emily gets favored because she's the oldest. I guess that explains a lot of why you act like you do. And the oldest does tend to take over and decide things. That happens in every family. But it sounds as if maybe now you can yield to each other a little bit."

Gardner: "What's yield?"

Mother: "Well, you know when we're driving and

two streets are coming together and there's a yellow sign that says YIELD? That means if somebody's driving along the other street, I have to slow down to let him go first."

Emily: "But how can we each let the other one go first?"

Mother: "Well, that would be a different kind of problem than each wanting to be first, that's for sure! But even when there are yield signs, it doesn't mean everybody obeys them. That's why they have traffic policemen who have to give out tickets. At least we've got a start toward working it out over Fido, and you know how the other one feels about things and why there are so many fights. I don't think we'll have a problem with everybody wanting the other one to go first. But maybe it's time to take turns—first the oldest and then the youngest. That would begin to take some of the sharp edges off fighting because everyone wants to be first all the time."

The Family Map

I certainly don't suggest that there are pat formulas for finding out more about the rivalry between your children and working toward better solutions. Every situation is different; you can invent your own practice and negotiation methods. The techniques in this book are only meant to stimulate your own ideas and help you find what works for you. Whatever you do, it's helpful to get beyond the outside layer of fighting and see what lies inside. It's like peeling off the layers of an onion, painstakingly, one at a time, gradually getting to know the emotional lives of your children better, not just as individuals, but how they behave as a group. The sum of the parts doesn't represent the whole. The back-and-forth give-and-take between them (and you) adds an extra dimension, and you can learn a lot from it. It's always wise to find out about your kids' relationships to you as well as to each other. Here's how a parent did exactly that, using a family map to find out where everybody stood.

Ask Not for Whom the Bell Tolls

The Walters family was starting a two-week summer vacation. Barbara and Eric Walters had two children, Eric, Jr., seven, and Ellen, six. They had half a day's driving left to get to the lake and the cottage they'd rented. After a couple of hours of sitting together in the back seat, the children were at each other's throat.

Eric: "Mommy, she took my window."

Ellen: "Because if we pass any cute animals like deer and bears, you can only see them from this side."

Father: "You children cut it out! I'm driving and have to concentrate on the road. I mean it!"

Barbara: "Cut it out now, children. Why don't you play with the games I got for you?"

Eric: "Because she cheats and besides she took my coloring book!"

Ellen: "You drank my root beer!"

There was a truce for another ten minutes. Then the war erupted again.

Eric: "Mommy, she's stretching out on the seat and I don't have any room."

Father: "I want you both to stay on your own half of the back seat and not cross over the line!"

Ellen: "Mommy, he's got his foot over the bump on the floor. Stop it! You're touching me!"

Barbara: "Maybe I should get in the back seat and split them up."

Father: "That only works for a while. Then they complain even more."

Barbara: "I think we'll have to get Daddy earplugs or tie up you children. He's about had it with you."

Father: "That's right. I think I'll stop the car and give you kids a good spanking if I hear one more sound."

Barbara: "Listen, dear, I've had experience driving a car pool with a bunch of kids cutting up in the back seat. Let me drive. It's my turn anyway."

Father: "Okay."

Father becomes navigator. He's much more relaxed with the children. As he takes the map from the glove compartment, he suddenly gets an idea. "You know, I've been looking at this map we got for our trip. Look, kids, here's the lake and here's where we are now. And, see, that's where home is. That's where we started out. Now I have an idea for a new game. It's a map game! Why doesn't everyone draw a map of our family?"

Ellen: "How do you do that?"

Father: "Well, here's a piece of paper and a pencil. And here's one for you too, Eric. Each of you draw a circle for everybody in the family, one for Mommy, one for me, one for yourself, and one for each other. Put them anyplace on the paper you want. Put them where you think they belong, next to each other or farther away, and then we'll compare maps. I'll do one too."

Each does one except Mother who's driving. When they're completed, they're passed around. Father compares them and finds that there is a similarity between the drawings of the children. The circle representing Father is off to one side of the page. The children and their circles are straddling Mother who's in the middle as if each is trying to pull her in a different direction. Each of the children drew his or her circle larger than the other and the mother circle larger than the father circle.

They all pass the slips of papers around and begin to talk about how it looks like they're fighting to be first with Mom and how Dad is on the outside. Getting the window, more room in the seat, and other things seem to be the way they show this. Father asks why he's outside the main group in their drawings. He had drawn himself and Mother together, and the kids together beneath the larger twin circles.

Eric: "That's the way you'd like it, Dad. And maybe that's why you holler at us when we really aren't doing anything."

Mother: "Sometimes I think I fall in with it. I let them break up our partnership and take sides with them and you get to be the bad guy. It backfires, though, because then they fight over me when they think they've gotten you out of the picture. Maybe at the lake we can do more things with them and get you back in the center of the page. Then they'll be together as brother and sister instead of split up over me. Let's see what the family maps look like when we do it again later."

At the lake, Father realized he did little but say "Don't do this" and "Don't do that" to the children. If he was unavailable, no wonder they fought for Mother all the time—she was the only one left. So he took the kids fishing and taught them to sail and really enjoyed it. When they got home he decided it was silly not to be a part of his kids' lives just because he didn't particularly like to play children's games or read stories. So he let them in his workshop and let *them* join *him*. They loved it. They learned to use drills and saws and before long were helping him fix things. Then, with scraps of lumber, they built some simple toys and finally a small table.

One evening, they said, "Let's draw a family map like we did on the trip." All the maps had mother and father circles together and the children together as well. Each child circle was still bigger than the other. What do you expect? Miracles? The family realignment was the important thing.

Using the Paradox

A paradox is defined by the dictionary as "an assertion or sentiment seemingly contradictory, or opposed to common sense, but that yet may be true in fact." Sometimes you can help children take a look at themselves in the mirror of their infantile behavior by letting it continue, indeed, even encourage it to the point where they suddenly see it as ridiculous and absurd.

This has to be done very carefully or it becomes harmful. It should never be done in a sarcastic or sadistic way. For example, the old stories of youngsters who were caught smoking behind the garage and were then forced to smoke the entire pack of cigarettes until they were sick were a misuse of the idea. Or telling them to "go ahead, fight it out" encourages further aggression (the physical way of dealing with problems) rather than moving toward mental or intellectual resolutions. Furthermore, it can be physically harmful and psychologically damaging if the stronger sibling winds up completely dominating the other. Used carefully, the paradox can be a useful technique. It does need a family with a good sense of humor to work.

Cinderella

Tommy, the youngest, is complaining about his brother, as usual. "How come I do all the work in the yard and he doesn't do any?"

Mother: "Because you're like Cinderella, the one who deserves to do all the work and not have any fun. Let me think of some more work. You don't have enough!"

Tommy: "And he gets more things than I do."

Mother: "Of course, dear, we give him everything we

can and try hard not to give you anything! Only once in a while we slip up and make a mistake."

Tommy: "How come he gets away with everything? You love him more than me! I know it."

Mother: "Of course we do. He's so lovable we let him do anything he wants and we don't want you to have any fun. You'd be spoiled! Besides, we hate you. You know that. We certainly try hard to be mean to you, Tommy, you've got to admit that, don't you?"

By now Tommy is breaking up laughing: "Okay, forget it. I guess sometimes I get a little, how do you say, paranoid?"

The humor soon gets through. The youngster sees how his angry "victim" position becomes absurd when it's exaggerated by Mother. She agrees with his complaints and carries them further instead of trying to counter them with rational arguments—the reaction that Tommy wants.

Some families have used this technique for children who're angry and out of control. Parents may put the kids in a room and tell them to continue to scream or hit a punching bag or a BoBo doll until they've gotten it out of their system. But I hesitate to recommend this: sometimes children get more out of control and *don't* get it out of their system, if only because there's no adult around to help. So they get more and more frightened of not being able to handle themselves. If you're determined to try this scheme, use it very cautiously.

Here's another example of the paradox: actually prescribing the behavior you want to eliminate until the kids are saturated with it and want to stop.

The Case of the Messy Room

Cynthia and Susie shared a bedroom. Space was limited, and their mother felt that the sharing was good practice in learning how to live with somebody else. Sharing a room would help prepare them for going to camp in the summer, for college, even for marriage. But Cynthia was constantly complaining that Susie messed up the room and didn't pick up after herself. Cynthia was right. She yelled at Susie constantly, but Susie pretended indifference or ignorance except for some complaining to Mother when Cynthia went too far and threw her clothes out the window or hit her.

One day Mother got tired of hearing this broken record over and over again. She said, "Susie, Cynthia says you're too messy. I can't believe it could be *that* bad. So let's see how messy you can really be. Today I want to see how much you can mess up the room. Really, do the best job you possibly can. And, Cynthia, you keep screaming at her. Scream as loud as you can and as often as you can. But don't pick up after her."

The two girls laughed. They thought Mom had flipped. For the next day, Susie "tried" to be messy, dropping dirty clothes all over. Finally, she ran out and emptied her drawer of clean clothes. Cynthia yelled and screamed at her between giggles. Before bedtime, they came downstairs and Cynthia said, "Mother, stop it. It's silly. Susie knows how messy she is and she's had enough. She wants to stop. And I heard myself yelling; it sounded really stupid. We've got a new deal about picking up."

If you can separate the antagonism and anger of fighting from the "act" of the fighting itself, you can see the "fight" out of its usual context and it becomes absurd. The girls exaggerated and mirrored their own behavior and decided they had had enough. Sensibly, they could then decide to break their old patterns and reorganize their attitudes toward themselves and each other.

Learning to Negotiate

Another skill for separating anger from fighting (so it can be examined) is negotiation. If youngsters are to grow up and recognize that their own needs, particularly immediate needs, can't be satisfied all the time, they must learn how to compromise—the earlier, the better.

It can be taught. Some famous attorneys grew up in families where they were forced to be negotiators between warring parties, usually parents. This is negotiation for the sake of one's own survival, hardly the best way to learn. It is better if you pick up this skill as a natural by-product of watching people live together. Negotiating requires the capacity to imagine alternatives. This is too much to ask of young children. Their minds can't handle several similar possibilities at one time. For the first few years, only one way of doing things (the way that most quickly satisfies one's wants) is imaginable. Younger children have to be offered alternatives over and over again until they develop the ability to think of them and weigh them as their own.

The Tower of Babel

Carolyn, five, and Ray, four, are playing on the kitchen floor with their blocks. Each is building a tower. Ray has run out of blocks. He takes one from Carolyn's tower, knocking it over. Carolyn kicks Ray's tower, then hits him for good measure.

Mother has seen what happened and stops the fight. She decides to make a lesson out of it and says, "Ray, you needed another block and just grabbed it from her tower. Then she broke your tower and hurt you. Is there another way you could have gotten a block if you needed one?"

Ray: "I could have hit her first and then took it."

Mother: "Yes, that's another way and I'm glad you can think of something else." Mother obviously wanted to continue the conversation, so she didn't fault Ray for this idea. If she had, it might have gone no further. At least he was trying to consider alternatives, primitive though they might be.

"There's another way, Ray, and I'll tell it to you so you can remember it: you could ask her for it, and maybe if you said, 'please,' she'd let you use it."

Ray: "But what if she didn't want to give it to me?"

Mother: "You'd be disappointed and then you might take it anyway. But don't worry if asking for something right away doesn't always work. You could ask to use it later, when she's finished. She'd probably say OK to that. There's another way, too. You could decide to build a tower together! Then everybody would have more blocks. You could ask to help with her tower or ask her to help with yours. Then you'd need to take turns."

Mother is trying to develop the ability to imagine several possibilities for Ray. She's also bringing in another way to play—cooperative play—a step beyond their accustomed parallel play. If you do this over and over again so the kids get plenty of alternative experiences and, eventually, more chances of getting satisfaction, you're on the right track. As youngsters get older, they'll develop more capacity for finding alternatives themselves.

Make a Wish

Richard, seven, and Billy, six, had been waiting for two whole days after Thanksgiving watching the turkey wishbone drying in the sun on the kitchen window. It was finally ready .

Mother: "Okay, each of you make a wish." Billy wished

for all the peanut butter in the world. Richard wished the president would say that kids didn't have to go to school when they didn't want to.

"Okay," said Mother, "pull." Crack. Billy won. Richard hit him in the throat with his fist. Mother said, "Richard, I'm ashamed of you! That's a terrible thing to do!"

Richard: "He cheated! Didn't you notice how he put his thumb near the bottom of the wishbone? That's the way you win."

Billy: "That's what you taught me to do!"

Mother: "Even if he did, hitting him right away wasn't the only way you could have handled it. Think of another way."

Richard: "Oh, I know. I could have told you he cheated so *you* could've hit him. But there's nothing else to do because the wishbone is all gone and there won't be another till next Thanksgiving. I hope he's dead by then!"

Mother: "Come on, Richard, think of another way, one more."

Richard: "Well, I guess I probably could give him a warning. Like sticking a pin in him or something to warn him not to do it again. Then if he did it again, I could hit him. Better still, I could stop the wishbone pull if I noticed him cheating and ask you to be the judge."

At seven, Richard doesn't have to be told all the alternatives the way Ray did. He can work some out himself. They may not seem sophisticated to you but they're a step beyond settling everything physically. He is using intellectual resources to try to meet his mother's expectations that he can go beyond hitting. He can.

Sticking a pin in his brother doesn't get away from physical pain as a main ingredient of their relationship, but it does move hostilities into a warning stage. The next step for Richard is to find means to stand up for his own rights verbally and deal with his brother at the same time. He's figured out that he and Billy both want to win so badly they can't be objective. They need a third party who has no interest in the outcome to act as referee.

Contracts and Problem Solving

After age seven or eight, youngsters can learn to break down continual fights into smaller parts and begin to understand the reasons for them. And they can more than understand the reason for a fight. The really important objective is to learn what to expect from other people and what you have to give in return. When you build negotiation skills into relationships between brothers and sisters, each sibling's expectations and promises—i.e., the "contract" between them—can be spelled out. When people use different contracts and don't know it, they get in trouble.

Let's imagine your children sit down to play cards. They deal out the whole deck and divide it into a pile on each side. But one thinks the game is War and the other one thinks it's Slapjack. Each lays down a card from the top of his pile but there's no agreement about a rule to determine who wins the trick. Naturally, a fight begins. Getting them to agree that the game is War *or* Slapjack, but not both, will end that fight. It was a misunderstanding that needed to be brought out into the open.

Wouldn't it be nice if your children had a contract with each other that spelled out exactly what one expects from the other and gives in return? It could be much like the one you get from the appliance store when you buy a television set. Your service contract specifies how long you'll be guaranteed free labor and repairs, what kind of repairs, and how much you pay for this service if it is not included in the price of the set. You're much less likely to get into an argument with the store if eventualities are spelled out.

I know it really isn't possible for siblings to develop such a push-pull-click-click relationship with each other; it isn't even necessarily desirable. After all, human relationships in a family go beyond the mechanics of the business world where no basis exists for mutual trust. People who don't know each other need a contract. Still, the principle can be useful. It can take a vague, poorly defined, hostile atmosphere, punctuated with attacks and counterattacks, and break it down into a smaller, better defined set of expectations that are mutually agreed upon. That's bound to make relationships more manageable.

Common ground of agreement is the key. But before you can focus on agreed-upon expectations, you have to get rid of hidden ones that cause fights. Each youngster may be operating with unrealistic expectations. He or she may be only partly aware of them. Still, he or she constantly reacts with frustration because they can't be met. That's why fights pop up over and over again for seemingly little or no reason. The reasons are hidden. So first you need to get them out in the open.

It's such a simple idea. Often, though, we don't help them to get their likes and dislikes out in the open because we feel there's something basically wrong about family members feeling two opposite ways about each other. Still, it's a fact. And if *you* can accept the idea, you can go a long way toward helping *them* see that it's natural and normal.

You Tell Me Your Dream, I'll Tell You Mine

Mary Lou and Bob had two children, Jill, fourteen, and Billy, twelve. It seemed to Mary Lou and Bob that the children were always at each other. If one made chocolate chip cookies, he or she would always say to the other, "You can only have one." What an unnecessary statement! And invariably it provoked a fight.

The kids teased each other about girl friends and boy friends—neither having one but each loving to make the other uncomfortable by sensing an interest in somebody and broadcasting it to the world.

One day Mary Lou said, "I haven't heard you kids say one good thing about each other for months. I wonder if there's anything you really like about each other. And I wonder if you really know what you dislike about each other. You seem to jump on each other for whatever happens to come into your mind at the moment."

Jill: "Of course there are things we like about each other, Mother. You don't know anything."

Mother: "Well, if that's true, why don't each of you write down on one piece of paper eight or ten items that you like about the other and then eight or ten things you don't like about the other? I mean what the other does that bugs you the most. Then we can compare your lists and see if there's anything we could do something about. You might find whether there are some things that you really don't know about yourself that seem to be bugging the other."

Both children thought this was a good idea and for the next day each one worked on a top secret document about the other. They hadn't really thought about it before in that way. They certainly couldn't have sat down and discussed it. When they had to think about specific characteristics and behavior in the other, unexpected feelings began to surface. The next evening, they sat around the kitchen table after homework was done and compared lists.

Billy's list of Jill's "good qualities" read like this:

1. She lets me borrow her records and comic books. (She has the best collection I've seen.)
2. She's really smart. She gets good marks in school and the teachers all like her because she's smart. (Sometimes that bugs me, too.)
3. She helps me with my homework when I need help.
4. She compliments me when I do things well, like making cookies.

5. She tells me what her friends say about me, especially if it's not so hot.
6. She gives me advice on high school and other things that I haven't gotten to yet because I'm younger. It's like having someone giving you a head start on stuff you're going to run into so you won't have so many problems with them. She has it tougher being the oldest. She has to go first.
7. She's cute. All of my friends rate her ten out of ten.
8. She doesn't tell her friends that I'm a jerk and she doesn't tell them the dumb things I do.

Jill's list of "good qualities" in Billy:

1. He's a natural jock. He can do every sport. And he's a good dancer, for a boy.
2. I guess he's pretty cute. It's hard to judge since he's my brother, but I guess he's pretty good looking. Probably eight out of ten.
3. He can always cheer me up. He knows how to make me laugh.
4. I can count on him to tell me my faults truthfully, usually when no one else will. When I complain to Mom and Dad about my fat thighs, they tell me it's my imagination. Billy agrees with me—they are fat.
5. He gives me ideas about what clothes to wear.
6. He gives me ideas about what boys like. Usually he's understanding. He'll talk to me about problems like a good friend, especially when it's something Mom and Dad don't understand.
7. He makes great chocolate chip cookies.
8. He's honest (except playing Monopoly).

Jill said, "This is weird, I never listed things like that or heard somebody else list my good points."

Mother: "Well, you both came up with the same idea about the cookies Billy makes, that they deserved compliments. Which things did you know the other guy would put down and which ones were a surprise to you?"

Jill: "Well, I knew he liked to borrow my records and comics. But I didn't know he appreciated my helping him with his homework that much, 'cause he's always bragging about how easy it is. I liked that he realizes I don't go around talking behind his back to my friends about him, even though sometimes I threaten to when I'm really mad."

Billy: "I guess you're right about the cookies and compliments. We do like the same things sometimes. And the thing I didn't know was the same one she mentioned. That she thinks I'm honest and I don't run her down to my friends. But she lied about Monopoly. I don't cheat!"

Mother: "Wait a minute, we're getting into an argument! It's not whether you cheat or not, Billy, it's what she *thinks*, just like what you think about her. It sounds as if there's something you both have in common that you didn't realize before. That's a kind of loyalty to each other. You might fight a lot around the house, but outside you stick by each other with your own group of friends and don't run the other down. And there's something that I realized from your list that I didn't know before. Sometimes it seems to me that all you do is argue and fight. But there's something else going on I don't see, and that's that the two of you are good friends and confide in each other and rely on each other for opinions. You sure do a good job of hiding that from your Dad and me. Well, let's get into those *other* lists."

Billy's list of what he doesn't like about Jill:

1. She makes me take the trash out after dark a lot. It's her week to do it, but she says she's scared of the dark so I have to do it.
2. She's terribly bossy. She bosses me around all the time. But I guess that's what older sisters are like

because my friends say the same thing about theirs.

3. She grabs the *TV Guide* every Sunday first and circles programs she wants to watch. She cops it before I have a chance and blocks out practically the whole week.
4. She thinks she's foxy.
5. She scratches and pulls my hair during fights.
6. She keeps telling me that certain foods in the kitchen cupboard are hers. She says she bought them at the store, but it's really part of the family groceries because she didn't use her money. And she hoards and doesn't eat them herself, but she won't let me have any.
7. She goes in my room and takes my things when she can't get back at me for something she's mad at. She threw my tennis racket in the bushes just before a match I was in, and I was so upset I lost.
8. She's always brushing her hair. She brushes it at the table and in the bus going to school. And she brushes it right in my face!

Jill's list of things she doesn't like about Billy:

1. He picks his nose at the table when Mom and Dad aren't looking and then *examines* what he's found. And I sit across from him so I see it all the time.
2. He tries to act like a hood. He wants to prove he's strong so he starts fights. He says, "You do that one more time and I'll punch you," and pushes me up against the wall.
3. He knows my best defense is scratching when it comes right down to it. Actually, it's kind of pinching with my nails. And he knows he can punch me and I'll scratch back, and scratching shows up more than punching so I'm the one who gets in trouble.
4. He tries to be a goody-goody with Mom and Dad.

If I'm getting scolded, he takes sides in an argument I'm having with Mom that he has nothing to do with. He butts in just to get me mad. He says, "I would *never* do a thing like that. Jill shouldn't either, just like you said, Mom. No, I don't think you should let her watch the TV special either."

5. He *deliberately* does things he knows bug me—passes gas, burps, chews out loud, or makes gross sounds. Half the time he sounds like he's in labor.
6. I let him borrow my records and magazines and do a chore for him and he wouldn't let me wear his warm-up jacket or even touch his Earth Wind and Fire record or help me with a chore when I ask him—even when I ask him nicely.
7. He brags terribly (but not as much as he used to).
8. He watches totally stupid, lame, immature, baby shows on TV, like cartoons and "Wonder Woman," when there's a *good* show on another channel. But he gets there first.
9. When I'm watching a serious, emotional show on TV and it gets to a good part, he starts joking around, bounces his basketball, or something. He ruins the whole part and when I ask him to leave or shut up, he won't.

Billy and Jill had told each other in an organized (rather than accusatory) way what they were annoyed about. They were getting beneath the layer of fighting and arguing. The anger was separated from the fight. They'd broken fighting into its various components as seen from both sides. They began to discuss it—and that was perhaps the most important step. Lists by themselves don't do much good. But they can begin peace negotiations and lead to "contracts" based on needs, not misunderstandings or overexpectations.

Mother: "I guess when the youngest one thinks the oldest bosses him around a lot, all the youngest can do is to provoke and make things uncomfortable for the oldest. Maybe that's a problem that could be worked on. And then it sounds as if the oldest gets into more arguments with Mom and Dad, and that's a chance for the youngest to get back. How about taking one of the items both of you agree is a problem and trying to work it out? Just one thing at a time."

Jill: "Tell him not to push me around and punch me and I won't scratch him."

Mother: "That's not the point. We're not getting into the business of my telling you. What could the two of you work out together? Could each of you tell the other what you're willing to give and what you expect in return so you agree to the same contract?"

Billy: "I don't mind her using my jacket. I don't know why I wouldn't let her. From now on I will, in exchange for being able to use her records and comics. I didn't know she wanted my jacket. I mean, I guess I didn't realize that she ought to be able to use it because I use her stuff. But she better get more comics, because I'm getting tired of the old ones."

Jill: "I've told you a million times I'd like to use your jacket because it's cool. [It was a Christmas present from parents.] And there's no reason not to let me."

Mother: "That's just what he said."

Jill: "Getting back to the scratching. I mean it really isn't scratching; it's just pinching and I only do it when I'm in trouble."

Billy: "Oh, brother! How about those red streaks down my arm that *bleed?* And besides, I don't punch you first. Yesterday I punched you because you were stretching my shirt, grabbing and pulling on it."

Jill: "I don't do things like that! I never!"

Billy: "Oh, then why does my shirt look like it was made for an elephant?"

Jill: "I wanted to wear one of your shirts."

Billy: "Then why don't you ask for it nicely instead of trying to take it off my back? I might say yes."

Mother: "It sounds as if you're getting someplace, arguing things out and bargaining and negotiating. Is there any particular fight you might work on, something that you both see as a problem? How about television?"

Billy: "No, that's not a problem."

Mother: "Well, it seems to be from her point of view and from yours, too. But maybe you can get to that later. There's another one, though."

Jill: "You mean chores?"

Mother: "Yes."

Billy: "Okay, let's try to work out some rules about chores and what each of us expects to do and the other one to do."

Jill: "Rule number one is 'Do your own chores and don't complain about them.'"

Billy: "Okay, rule number two is 'If someone spends the night or weekend at a friend's house, then the other one does their chores and they'll repay you the same way when you stay over.'"

Jill: "No, that's not fair—you stay overnight more than I do."

Billy: "But even if it doesn't even out exactly, it's an agreement to take care of it for each other. How about 'Always ask and don't order when it's time to do chores'?"

Jill: "No, that's your way of criticizing me. How about 'Do chores on time because it's easier'?"

Billy: "Okay. How about 'Don't complain about being nagged by Mom to do them because it's your own responsibility'?"

Jill: "Okay, agreed. Let's try those rules this week."

Mother: "That's a pretty good set of rules to work on. I've been writing them down like a regular contract. Both of you read it and sign it if you agree. I'll sign as a witness and we'll post it on the refrigerator door for a week."

Finally, "Billy, you mentioned having to take the trash down for her if it's dark. You really don't have to. It's her job. I wonder if you do it because you sympathize with her or because you make a deal about something else. You complain about her bossing you around but you fall in with it."

Jill: "I'm not going to boss him around anymore if he does things like that for me. At least I'll try. Let's see the contract."

As you can see, beginning with an understanding of how each perceives the other, then dividing the perceptions into good and bad qualities, gives kids a baseline for understanding each other better. It not only pinpoints the viewpoints of each, uncolored by the anger that goes with the fighting; it can also detect what each was (or wasn't) aware of, even though siblings know each other very well, better than you do. It also points up unrealistic attitudes of the relationship. Given workable rules and opportunity, they can identify things about each other, read each other's mind, in a way you never can. It may be quite a surprise to you.

Moving from that point to common agreements around particular problems, one at a time, can lead to negotiation between the siblings themselves. The contract really depends on what each one expects from the other and what each one promises to give in return. It isn't merely a one-for-one favor exchange. It is really the development of a total relationship which goes on and on. The parts become mixed together again once they've been separated. It's like the flow of a river. It may start with a single contract. It becomes a continuing, evolving quid pro quo that sharpens sights about what to expect. It lessens surprises, disappointments, anger.

As you can see, this is a mix of the stages in the developmental section: You Scratch My Back and I'll Scratch Yours;

It's not Fair, You're Cheating—The Law and Order Stage; and a bit of the fourth stage, As Brothers and Sisters Go, You're Not So Bad, a drop or two of altruism.

A few weeks later Billy and Jill were beginning to feel that each could trust the other a little more, that what one gave to the other would be gotten back eventually. They were settling things themselves. It was a long process from the time they were preschoolers and Might Equals Right needed Mother to settle things for them. It had worked because their parents shifted their approach each time they saw a chance. They didn't stay in the Might Equals Right stage; they knew it was only temporary and would never solve things in the long run. Billy and Jill put it very well when Jill said, "You know, Mom, when you and Dad holler at us to stop fighting or to get along with each other, it really doesn't help at all. It just unites us. It brings us together against the two of you."

Billy: "And if it does look like we've stopped fighting, we really only did for a few minutes so you can't see. It really doesn't stop anything going on between us. We have to work it out ourselves."

Listen to the popular comedian Bill Cosby. He recalls his own sibling rivalry in a way that makes us laugh because it touches us all. He and his little brother Russell lie in bed at night teasing, threatening, scaring each other. They have water fights and pillow fights. They're terrified of their father who periodically comes in and shouts "Quiet!" The fighting goes on. It only stops when Father is physically present. The presence has no lasting effect. Bill Cosby solved his sibling rivalry. He made it live on to entertain the child in us all.

IV

SPECIAL SITUATIONS

The Christmas Holidays

Certain festivals are supposed to represent the happiest memories of childhood because children get so much special and extra attention. But for some reason the holiday spirit often goes awry and fighting increases between brothers and sisters. Why?

Because these times are loaded emotionally. They bring into the open children's wishes to have more than each other—more material things and more love from parents. Don't forget this is an underlying reason for sibling rivalry throughout the year. So you can easily understand how it can become more difficult to control at these special times. The delicate emotional balance between brothers and sisters is upset by the heightened excitement. On top of that, special expectations—ones they can't meet—overload the kids' circuits.

One of the most common is "being good" for Christmas.

'Tis the Season to Be Jolly, Tra La La La La . . .

Mr. and Mrs. Baker took their two preschoolers, Christine and Bobby, to see Santa Claus at the shopping mall. They waited for over an hour. The youngsters were crying, pulling on Mother's skirt, and screaming, "Let's go home." Bobby wet his pants. Mrs. B. was exasperated. *They* were the ones who'd insisted on coming. But logic wasn't the answer. They were overtired, had waited too long, and the stress of the Christmas season was showing on everyone.

While Mrs. Baker was trying to decide what to do, the problem was solved. They arrived at the throne. Chris was on Santa's knee. "Ho, ho, ho, my little girl, what can Santa bring you for Christmas?" Chris answered, "A pony. That's what I really want." "Oh, oh," said Father, "now what're we going to do? The problem is what they wish for and what we can actually give them. They're *bound* to be disappointed."

Next, Santa had Bobby on his lap. "Have you been a good boy this year?" Santa asked. Mrs. Baker whispered to her husband, "I never really thought about it before, but that's an awfully silly question. If Bobby says yes, he's bound to feel guilty about lying because nobody's been good for the whole year. That just rubs it in. If he tells the truth and says no, he's liable to get mad at himself *and* Santa for making him confess and then take it out on us!"

Bobby dutifully said, "Yes," got down from the throne with the trinket he'd picked from Santa's bag, and began comparing it with the toy Chris got. Each was unhappy and felt the other had gotten a bigger or better one.

"We'll, that's par for the course," said Mr. B. "I guess we should just allow for it."

"And it's probably a preview of coming attractions Christmas morning," said his wife. On the way out she said, "The whole season peaks too early. But there's nothing I can do about it. Even when I try to set up our *own* timetable before Christmas, the rest of the world won't let me. I have to have the packages wrapped and at the post office by November 15 if they're going to reach the folks on time. Seeing all that wrapping paper and those presents lying around at home gets the kids in the mood. And the constant ads and reminders on television! And the decorations on the street and in the stores! Everything seems to start earlier and earlier every year. The kids just can't tolerate such a long time of having to be good and not being able to because we get them so excited. The reading on their greed scale must be over a hundred! And I'm not sure we're any different, having to be happy and generous such a long time."

Mr. B.: "Yeah, and did you notice how their preschool stepped up the kids' production of finger painting and clay paperweights before we start the season? Even if the quality of their work goes down, it has to be cranked out for the relatives. If I hear Chris threaten one more time not to give me the present she made me at school I think I'll tell her to donate it to the Smithsonian!"

Mother: "Wait till Christmas morning. We're *really* Santa. If she doesn't get that pony, the store Santa won't be around to catch it for not meeting her hopes. It'll be us! The kids seem to lose all perspective at Christmas about what's possible. Well, here's the car. Let's get these two home for Christmas Eve. It's not really their fault they're fighting more. We've upset the apple cart with too much Christmas spirit, even though we complain about it, too."

In the car, Bobby was crying and kicking his sister. Wham! She hit back. Mother asked, "What's the matter, kids?"

He sobbed, "She had fun and I didn't."

Mother: "That's the trouble with Christmas, I guess. You think everybody else is having such a good time and you're not."

Turning to her husband, she said, "You know, I think the reason I always get a little blue around Christmas is that it brings back the same kind of memories to me— that my brothers and sisters were having a good time and getting more than I was."

Father: "Mostly what people remember about Christmas is what they wanted and didn't get, not what they got."

That night they all had fun decorating the tree and singing carols, especially the two older boys, John and Teddy. The presents were laid out after the children went to bed. Chrissy and Bobby would get several identical presents to try to minimize jealousy and fighting. All told, there were three or four duplicate gifts and one or two different ones that the kids had specifically requested. Mr. and Mrs. Baker had also noted some things the kids wanted during the year and had bought them then. The idea was not to have to crowd everything into a few short weeks of wishing and buying. In addition to the sled, the football, a ballerina doll, and the stuffed shaggy dog (as big as a real one), there was a set of puppets, a surprise experiment with one present that needed some degree of cooperative play to be fun.

They put the presents on separate chairs, each young-ster having an assigned place. The two older boys each had one "big" present: a new bike and a remote control gasoline-powered model airplane. The Bakers were ex-hausted but happy. They didn't know that both boys were crouching on the stairway.

"Shh," said John, "they'll hear us. I told you there wasn't any Santa Claus; it's really Mom and Dad."

Teddy said, "I knew it all the time. Remember last Easter? I was the one who kept us awake all night by singing so we could see who the Easter Bunny was. You fell asleep and I saw Mom and Dad bring in the baskets of candy to put under our beds. And they thought I was asleep!"

I Come First, You Come Third

Much later, while Teddy *was* asleep, John sneaked downstairs. It was 3:00 A.M. He examined his presents laid out on the sofa and compared them with Teddy's. He changed a few and went back to bed. The alarm rang at 6:00 A.M. and they all raced downstairs. Chrissy and Bobby were playing with their duplicate toys.

Teddy said, "I didn't want this Luke Skywalker X-Wing Fighter model kit. I wanted Darth Vader's Ti-Fighter. That's what I asked for. I hate Santa!"

Chrissy said, "Don't be mad, Teddy, I begged Santa for a pony and look what I got instead—a rubber ducky!! You got better stuff than I did."

Father smelled a rat. The models were similar, but he remembered where they'd placed each box and who'd asked for which. "John, are you sure Darth Vader is yours?"

John replied, "Well, Teddy would probably want to trade with me anyway. He always wants the stuff I get. Don't you, Teddy?"

Teddy: "I hate Santa."

John: "There is no Santa, you turkey!"

By this time, they were pushing each other and had knocked some ornaments off the tree.

Mother said, "John, my guess is you have a guilty conscience about something" (thinking to herself that he really deserved Darth Vader—they were cut of the same cloth!). "And both of you seem mixed up about Santa. If you don't think there's a Santa, then who is it?"

John: "It's you guys!"

Mother: "Then I guess you're really fighting with each other over us and what we gave each of you. You've just learned something: that Santa is really your parents showing their love for you, but you don't even have faith that we love you both. Do you really think we'd favor one over the other?"

Teddy: "I don't care. Santa Claus is just a trick made up by parents. I'm going to tell Chrissy and Bobby."

Mother: "Just because you each *think* your brother got

something better than you did, you're mad at Santa and us. And you want to take it out on the little ones. But honest—we really love you all."

John: "Don't worry, Teddy's just mad. I'm going to trade models back. Santa's not a trick. It's a good thing to believe in, especially for the little kids. Teddy, let's not take Santa away from them. They'll learn by themselves."

Teddy: "Okay."

Rivalry between the two older boys had been reduced to its basic element—their expectation and uncertainty about Santa really reflected their concern about their place with their parents. Both were reassured at least temporarily when the true issue was talked about in the open. They even formed a partnership with their parents to keep Santa alive as long as the younger kids wanted it.

Children *do* want it when they're young. It's just a big jolly parent in disguise. There's no harm in it. If you think about it, you've probably told them worse fibs. John and Teddy decided not to disillusion the little ones—could this be an act of consideration toward siblings? Sure, friendship and kindness is easiest toward the younger ones—the real competition was with each other.

The Christmas Hangover

Finally, late in the day, Christmas dinner was over. Grandparents and a bachelor uncle were there. The Bakers were washed out. It had been a long Christmas Day. The children were overexcited by too many toys strewn around the floor. Chrissy's imitation pearl necklace broke and the pearls were everywhere! The younger kids had spent much of the day opening a present, holding it momentarily, then dropping it to see what the other one had. A rationing system of presents went into effect to slow this competition down.

Dinner had been a mess. The young ones were overtired and didn't eat their turkey. Having to make table conversation with grandparents was just too much for them. Long-distance phone calls from relatives had interrupted the dinner twice so even the older ones were poking at each other. It was hard for the Bakers. They had to be parents to their own children—and children to their own parents, all at the same time.

The children were finally excused from the table, but Teddy was in tears. His gasoline-powered remote control model airplane wasn't assembled. It was still in the box. Everyone had been too busy—Mother cooking dinner, Father entertaining her parents and his brother—to help Teddy put it together.

Father: "I'll help you tomorrow, son. John, why don't you help him?"

John: "I'm going out to ride my new bike."

Grandfather, realizing the grown-ups had made themselves a separate group from the children, broke it up: "I'll help you, Teddy. In fact, I think we can get it together before dark, in time to take it out for a test run." He'd noticed that while Teddy was surrounded by a three-ring circus of toys, his main present, the remote control plane, was unusable. Besides, it was really human companionship that he needed. He was lonely, angry, and unhappy. He and Grandfather went to work. They pretended they were the Wright brothers.

I don't mean to debunk Christmas; its problems aren't its fault. On the contrary, there's tremendous value in holidays such as Christmas. They can heighten religious experience and reinforce the sense of belonging to a family. Their festive atmosphere makes for easy release of tension. We can surprise other people and be closer to them, even if only briefly.

But more goes on: old feelings and memories about our own early family life and sibling relationships come back to haunt us, especially when our own family is around to rub it in and remind us of what we really were like when we were young! There's also something artificial about the sentimentality of a family reunion when it's all crammed into one or two days a year. It's too much stress on everyone.

Having to give gifts to people as an obligation (rather than a sign of genuine affection) seems to be the adult version of sibling rivalry. The jokes about mother-in-law ties are perhaps the best example—presents are just a bit off the mark; still, they're presents so you have to be grateful.

Another thing: we expect ourselves and others to be happy and generous all throughout the season. No wonder there's a letdown on Christmas Day! You've been dripping with love seventy-five times an hour (and the speed limit is only fifty-five!). Now you feel like a heel because you just don't have any more to give. You can only manufacture so much.

What's the answer? Don't expect to be a magician and make everybody happy. If you try beyond what's possible, you'll build up so much pressure inside you'll feel like a walking nervous breakdown. Instead, allow for a bit *more* irritability; it's tax exempt for yourself *and* the children at Christmastime. Be aware that you're in one of those life situations when you're supposed to be happy even though you're probably going to be plenty angry.

Do think of yourself, not just others. Sleep late, go to a movie, enjoy the New Year's Eve party. That's what it's for. Taking care of yourself and indulging yourself is one way to cure a feeling of being depleted. Not having enough is part of what comes back to haunt us all at Christmas.

The most obvious pleasure for all of us is to watch the excitement in our children—their breathless, wide-eyed surprise and squeals of pleasure in the Christmas tree and opening presents. The jealousy that erupts at least to some degree as they begin to get worn down by the prolonged Christmas spirit is inevitable. Remember, behind the fighting and arguing, partly produced by excess excitement, too many new things all at once for the body's system to absorb, is the fear of not having as much as the others, not being as important, not being loved as much by the parents.

It's as if youngsters are looking for proof that this fear is legitimate. That's why they compare presents microscopically and estimate their cost, to prove they came out on the short end.

Do realize that their fighting, strange as it may seem, serves a purpose. It wards off the sense of loneliness and worthlessness that everyone fears. Look at it this way: if you blame others for having more, you don't have to think about having less and about what this indicates about your own value. So be understanding; allow an increase in the barometer of rivalry; minimize it by spreading out the opening of presents over hours or even days, one or two at a time. Keep presents as similar as possible, especially for very young children, except when you *know* they want something because they've asked for it; if they get something they really want they won't care as much what brother or sister got.

And do give all the reassurance and affection you can. Toys don't substitute for your attachment to the children, doing things with them. Grandfather realized this when he saw poor Teddy sitting helplessly with the present he wanted the most, unable to use it because no one would help him put it together. John had even tried to exchange a present with Teddy who was younger. He wanted first choice, not taking any chances. Fortunately, his parents had two eyes and changed this arrangement. They didn't howl as if he'd hijacked an armored car; they also didn't ignore it and didn't allow him to blackmail Teddy into trading presents with him.

Birthdays and Birthday Parties

Making a birthday successful means making the birthday child feel special. It also means the balance between the siblings tilts like a seesaw. The kids see a sudden shower of attention and presents out of nowhere. The worst part is that the presents are brand *new*. A day or two later they'll blend into the family background. But on the birthday they're so shiny, and that makes a huge difference. It's as if the new toys add value to one child at the expense of the others so the others feel they're worth less. It's like the Aga Khan who used to be worth his weight in diamonds.

Jack and Jill Went Up the Hill . . .

The party was over at five o'clock. All the parents had picked up the visiting children. The kitchen and dining room tables were a mess—cake and ice cream, the clown centerpiece, paper hats and horns all mixed in a glubby mass with crepe paper streamers hanging over the edge like legs on an octopus. Mother had done her best. It was Tommy's ninth birthday, not Joan's. Joan was allowed to invite a friend to keep her company, but Tommy was to be special because it was his day. Mother had thought Joan agreed. But now the kids were wrestling on the floor, strewn with ribbon and birthday wrappings. Zonk! Joan screamed as he pulled her hair.

Tommy: "I'll teach you to ruin my new Hot Wheels car! Now it won't work!"

Mother: "What happened?"

Joan, seven: "I just wanted to try out the car on the rug because it's new. I didn't mean to hurt it. Besides, he has so many other things."

Tommy: "But that's my biggest present, and now the threads from the rug are in the wheels and the car won't go down the track."

Mother: "We'll fix it, Tommy, don't worry. Joan is naturally a little jealous of all your shiny new things. She didn't *mean* to wreck the car; she was just trying it out."

Tommy: "Oh yeah? Then why did she tell me ahead

of time that I was getting a skateboard from Gramps? Some surprise!"

At that point, Mother decides not to try to arbitrate or explain. It didn't work. She'd listen and let them air their gripes: "Go ahead, what else went wrong?"

Tommy: "She brought Gloria, a guest of *hers*."

Joan: "Mommy and Daddy said I could have some-body to play with."

Tommy: "But not a guest I didn't even invite. At least I could have had something to do with inviting her. And here she shows up with this dumb Tonka toy. Why couldn't they both go over to *her* house? Did they have to play pin-the-tail-on-the-donkey with us? And the two of them following us around everywhere—they were peeking when the boys were in the bathroom."

Joan: "You and your friends scared us at my birthday when we were sleeping outside in the tent. You kept making sounds like animals grunting and wouldn't let us alone."

Mother: "So you were getting back at him?"

Joan: "Yes, my friends all said, 'Oh, he's so cute, let him join us,' but his friends wouldn't let me join them. Or he wouldn't."

Mother: "I guess it's awfully hard to share a birthday with a brother or sister. Tommy, let's get the car fixed. And then, when you're playing with the set, Joan and I will go in the other room and begin to plan her birthday. I know it's a few months off, Joan, but you can make a list of presents you'll want to ask for. And let's try some-thing else next time. Tommy, how would you like to pick out a movie and we'll treat you and a friend to it during Joan's birthday party?"

Tommy: "Yeah, I'd like that. I think a birthday ought to belong to one person and not have to be shared. Today should have been my day."

Mother: "Okay. So if you decide at the last minute you

want to stay for Joan's party, and it's okay with her, maybe you shouldn't be her brother all day. You could pretend to be a guest like everybody else. Then you could enjoy the party and be part of it, instead of getting jealous the way Joan was getting today. Let's plan it that way for next time."

Tommy: "I'll even buy her a present and maybe I'll come in disguise under a different name! Then I can really feel like a guest instead of her brother!"

Planning for a future birthday with the other child often takes the edge off the jealousy or envy that naturally arises when a brother or sister has a birthday. Making out a future guest and gift list for the next party makes the other child feel important, too. It offers hope that the feeling of being one down to the birthday child will soon end. Some parents buy a small gift for the other children in the family who aren't having a birthday.

The main principle remains—the birthday child should feel special. Trying to make everyone perfectly happy just isn't possible. Balance—some attention and affection for the non-birthday child—may be helpful but should be kept separate from the main action, The birthday child shouldn't have to share the spotlight this one day of each year.

It's not just younger siblings who show envy and jealousy when the older has a birthday, so he now has even "more" and is getting "older" still. It works the other way, too. Believe it or not, the older child is often uncomfortable on the younger's birthday because of shadowy recollections of the younger one's birth. Whatever envy and jealousy was then set off may be re-aroused and flare up briefly.

On Joan's eighth birthday, Tommy wasn't able to carry off his plan to be just a "guest" rather than her older brother. He felt himself displaced once again, just as he had when she first came into the family. He thought to himself, *Why is everybody paying so much attention to her? What's so great about her?*

Some of the same techniques that minimize rivalry when a new baby comes into the home are sometimes useful. Mother decided that Tommy wasn't going to be a very good guest; he started violating house rules the night before by playing his records louder and louder, clearly a warning sign. So she asked him if he'd like to be a part of the birthday management. He did. He was very grown-up and helped her with the arrangements, with the cake, and with her supervision. He was the "bouncer" for problems when they got out of hand. He particularly liked being a part of the secret preparations. He was helping in the kitchen and Joan wasn't even allowed in.

So keep your options open. Be flexible. Be willing to shift gears as Tommy and Joan's mother did, trying to find the right answer for her nonbirthday child.

As you can imagine, twins have special problems with birthdays. During the rest of the year, identical twins often have fewer troubles about rivalry than natural brothers and sisters (as long as parents don't regard the twins as some special parental accomplishment). It probably helps that there is essentially no difference between them; they're mirror images, part of one another. They can often tolerate different toys early in life because they know they can trade with each other. It's as if they're still attached by a membrane and can flow back and forth between each other. That's not to say this is an advantage. It creates problems, too. But they may be hidden till later, as we will see.

Fraternal or nonidentical twins often encounter more difficulty and rivalry. Fraternal twins not only look different; they have different temperaments and are likely to clash more, like siblings very close in age. Identical twins look the same to outsiders but compare each other constantly; they know who's stronger, smarter. They're used to each other. In any event, for both kinds of twins, a birthday is a reminder of twinship and of fused identity.

Happy Birthday, Dear Twins, Happy Birthday to You

Betty and Debbie were identical twins. Their twelfth birthday was approaching. They were quarreling over plans for the party.

Debbie: "I don't want to go to the zoo. That's your choice."

Betty: "I don't want to go to that dumb movie you picked out."

Debbie: "I wish I wasn't a twin. The worst thing is you can't do anything about it!"

Betty: "We're not twins in personalities—you're a total slob and I'm neat! And I've been thinking—I'm going to move out of our room."

The parents were surprised; the twins had gotten along so well all their lives. They'd shared dollhouses, hamsters, bicycles, and games. They'd tolerated new shades of differences between them when they appeared. Now they were fighting over the invitation list for the party.

Mother: "I don't know why you're fighting over who's coming. You've got separate friends and we have separate invitation lists for each of you, plus a few kids you both want to invite. That's a *third* list."

Betty: "I don't like her friends! They're sloppy like she is. And I don't want her to use my clothes anymore."

Mother: "But you used to share clothes all the time."

Father: "I think they're getting to the point at age twelve that we saw in the other kids much earlier; they're fighting over differences. I don't think it'll be any worse than with the other kids; it's just a delayed reaction, that's all."

Mother: "We've always had two different cakes, and half of their presents have been the same and half of them different. I don't know what more we can do."

Father: "Why don't we try two parties? They could be

on either side of their birthday, or on a weekend, or on two different weekends. I can take one of them and her friends to whatever they want to do, a movie or the beach; you can take the other one and her group somewhere else."

Debbie and Betty agreed: "That's just what we want. It's time we were different from each other and everybody knew it."

It's hard for twins to relinquish being the center of attention because of their sameness. But they inevitably arrive at a point when they separate from each other. It may come early and it may come late. Here, arguing about the birthday party marks the beginning, at least the part the parents can see from outside. And Betty wants to move out of the room they shared all their lives. It's a good sign, and the parents responded positively to it, falling in with the pace the children had set.

Trying to separate them forcefully too early or promoting their single identity too long would mean resisting their *individual* developmental needs. They're experiencing the struggle to be individuals, to get away from sameness. They'll probably exaggerate the differences between them and become jealous of each other for a while. Don't worry that they might resent each other forever. The bond between twins is very deep. For now they need to separate, and their parents picked upon the birthday party as a sign of this need as well as a means for dealing with it.

Games and Toys

For adults, games are supposed to be relaxation. The challenge of doing well in the game should be satisfaction enough. Competition is fun; winning, while desirable, isn't always necessary. But children go through a long process to reach this point, and all the while their games are dead serious. Play is for youngsters what work is for grown-ups. Kids learn a good deal about life from learning to play, and you can learn a good deal about them from watching them play.

There are likely to be interruptions and breakdowns in their games, because they're learning how to channel their energy into the game, balancing the satisfactions of winning with the sadness and anger of losing. They're only gradually getting control over impulses that make them want to break loose and not be tied to silly rules that keep them from beating a sister or brother. Let's see how toys and games can be tailored to the kids' level of ability and interest, emotionally and physically.

Children for Rent—Make Offer

Mother had brought home a game of Pick-Up-Stix for Randy, eight. Randy wanted to try them out with his best friend next door but found he'd gone to see his grandmother. So Randy tried to interest his brother, Billy, five, and sister Jennifer, three. They began.

"Jennifer, you cheated—the red one moved!" Jennifer held the stick in her fist, having fun just moving the others around. She put some back in the tube and seemed more interested in doing that than playing the game. Billy tried a little harder. But he was having trouble, too. Billy tries to play the game but he's mad because the sticks keep moving on him. He shouts, "Stupid game!" and grabs a handful of sticks and throws them across the room. His sister does the same.

Randy, furious, is about to stab each of them with a stick when Mother bursts into the room, "Hold it! What's happened here?"

Randy says, "They've ruined my game, these dumb kids! Look what they've done! Now I'll never find all the sticks."

Mother untangles the children and gets the younger ones involved in something else. Then she and Randy pick up the sticks and she offers to play a game. Randy soon gets frustrated because she's winning. She stops the game.

"Randy, you know why I'm winning? It's easy. Not because I've played it a lot more than you and know the strategy better, but my hands are steadier because I'm older than you. You're getting upset because you're losing and can't do anything about it because of the difference between us. Now that's exactly how your sister and brother felt! Pick-Up-Stix isn't a game for little children or for kids of different ages to play together.

"There's an enormous difference between eight and three. You know that! You can hold a stick between two fingers and work it gently so it picks up the others. Your little sister can't even hold the stick the right way yet. Your brother can play it, but not as well as you because he's only five and his coordination isn't as good. Pick-Up-Stix is for kids who have about the same amount of coordination in their hands and fingers. Otherwise, somebody *always* wins and the other always loses and that's not good in any game."

Randy says, "You mean it's like when Dad bought me that model airplane last year for my birthday? He said he loved models as a boy and we tried to put it together. But I wasn't interested, I guess because I just couldn't follow the directions and work the little pieces into the right places and keep them glued together. Dad was disappointed, but I think he really got the model because *he* liked it."

Mother: "You know, he told me that himself afterward. He used to make models as a boy and forgot you were only seven. He really wanted to build them himself."

Mother realized that Jennifer was in the one- to three-year-old group where play is mostly solitary and, at best, parallel. Most of the time, youngsters of that age prefer to play alone.

When they want to play with Mother or brother or sister, they'll look for their company. It's important that at this early age they have simple toys and games that they can manage without anybody's interference. They don't need expensive toys. They're too complicated, too expensive, and parents are too worried about them getting broken!

Jennifer likes something she can step on, hit, and break open to see what's inside. She's learning to put objects in and out of containers. So toys have to suit that purpose. She was realizing how some things go inside other things and was excited with her experimenting. Finding out that she couldn't put a larger object inside a smaller one was an important lesson for her. That's why she was trying to put the sticks back in the box. It wasn't that she didn't want to play; *that* was her level of play. She had no interest in the object of the game. Randy was trying to make a three-year-old behave like one of eight. He didn't understand and got angry. Mother needed to separate their play "levels."

Billy, on the other hand, was five. The four- to six-year-old age group has become "cooperative"; they're *able* to play with others. But I'm sure you know that doesn't mean they *want* to. Problems are constant. Children at this age like rough-and-tumble play, so Pick-Up-Stix was a little beyond Billy and he tried to turn it into *his kind* of play, throwing things. (He was also frustrated by his inability to meet the object of the game, as Randy wanted.)

So four- to six-year-olds do best with free play that they can control, games they can make up and that let them use their bodies. Youngsters of this age love dramatic play—to dress up as a captain, a cowboy, a nurse, or just play Mother and Father. They'll make up stories and play roles based on what they've seen others do in real life or on television. Dressing up makes them feel big and allows them to imagine having adult powers. It gives them the right to act big, too.

Give them some hats and some of your old clothes, some big boxes or crates, and they can imagine a house, a castle, a ship, or a cave. Let their imaginations go. It's fun to be some-body scary, or Mommy or Daddy, or even the baby. Animal puppets, drawing, and clay or play dough give them a chance to be creative. Four- to six-year-olds can begin to shift to games (charades) that let them play animals and television charac-ters. They can also play board games if they're simple. The games should depend largely on luck, i.e., the spin of a pointer or the roll of dice. Younsters at this age are moving from physical ways of dealing with each other into a higher level, intellectual competition. Still, a good deal of luck should be left in the game during this transition period.

The first shift is physical, from using the whole body to using parts of the body, perhaps groups of muscles that require motor skill; the next shift is to intellectual and mathematical skills. With board games like Candyland, simple bingo, dice rolling, and such card games as Old Maid, Crazy Eights, Go Fish, War, Slapjack, they can learn to check the impulse just to take over and win. But remember, they're just *learning*.

You Broke My Funny Bone—It's Nothing to Laugh About

Billy, six, and Cindy, five, were playing Slapjack. Cindy was winning. Billy's slaps were getting harder and harder! Cindy slapped before her card was completely laid down. Billy had just enough patience to wait for the next Jack. Whack! She screamed and Mother burst into the room, feeling a little guilty because she should've checked now and then from the yard, just to keep things toned down by letting them know someone was there.

Cindy screamed, "He hit me so hard he broke my funny bone!"

Billy said, "She cheats, that's why she's winning! I just slapped her hand like I'm allowed to!"

Mother said, "Okay, we've got to go back to the two main rules again. First of all, you can't slap until the card is down. Second, you can't slap hard enough to hurt anybody." (Of course, there are other rules, such as only slapping Jacks or you're penalized, but these are the ones that are easy to accept and stick to.)

Mother: "I think you've probably had enough of this game. Let's try another one. How about Old Maid or Go Fish? Wait! I have a game for you that's a little harder. You spin for turns and you each have a piece that has to go around the board from start to finish. But in the middle you can get into all kinds of trouble. There are safe places, dangerous places, cards you have to take a chance on. It's really exciting. Let's try it all together and then see if the two of you can play it."

Billy and Cindy were still at the age when having a game determined by chance or luck wasn't good enough. They would still get into fights because they believed that somehow they should be able to control luck. If they got too far behind, the tension got too great to bear. But it was a shift toward higher-level games, using the mind more than the hands.

". . . And Where She Stops, Nobody Knows!"

Billy and Cindy loved the game. They played it over and over. And they played other games, too. One night Father looked up from his paper, saw Billy spin the pointer when it was his turn and then shout, "That didn't count—it didn't go around far enough!" Cindy: "You little cheat! Just because you got a two instead of a nine, you want to take it over."

Billy: "Don't call me a cheater! You jiggle the table whenever I'm spinning to make it stop where *you* want it."

Father had been doing his detective work. He knew that rolling dice and spinning pointers weren't the answer because sometimes the pointer landed on the line between "Go back two spaces'" and "Go forward five spaces." Then there was a real problem. Was it on the line? Then you should take the turn over. But usually the kids saw it more in the space they wanted. And sometimes there *was* a little table-jiggling to make it move. Anyhow, he saw the situation deteriorating. Soon it would be a physical contest again, and the original point of the game (to provide a higher level of competition) would be lost.

In a way he felt sorry for the kids. Their little hands and fists couldn't spin the pointer as easily as he could. He felt like letting them take a lot of turns over again, just to settle arguments. But that really wouldn't help; when they played with friends, what would happen if they always felt they had the right to take a turn over? It might make them feel better for the moment, but what would happen later?

He came out of his reverie when he saw Billy getting ready to hit Cindy over the head with the board. He knew the game had outlived its usefulness. Maybe the kids were ready to move on again. (Something new is usually exciting enough to get kids to cooperate for a while. It's only when they get bored with a game that the old jealousies begin to come out and cheating starts again.)

"Listen, you guys. You just can't change rules in the middle of a game and take another turn. You just can't, that's all. It isn't fair. Besides, this game is getting old. I think it's time to try a new one."

The next day he stopped on the way home from work and bought a game of Chinese Checkers. He remembered how much fun it had been when he was a kid. Also, it was a *different* game from the others.

"Okay, kids, let me show you how to set up this new game. You move your ten marbles across this board and whoever gets them all in the right places first wins. It takes a while. The different thing is, you jump your *own* marbles, too. And you don't take any marbles away from the other person."

Now he remembered: when he was a kid, playing regular checkers with his brothers always made him mad because you kept losing checkers. Somebody got to take somebody else's away all the time. That hurt. In Chinese Checkers, though, you were playing against yourself, trying to set up long complicated jumps. It took the sharp edge off just focusing on your opponent. The kids would soon find out there was no point trying to block the other pieces (which is awfully frustrating and hard to endure for long without blowing up), because it didn't pay. He and Mom could play, too. When you played partners, you *had* to learn to cooperate. It's more than just wanting to beat the other guy. Chinese Checkers was always a lot more fun than regular checkers. Why didn't kids play it more often these days?

After the age of seven, youngsters are ready for more advanced games. Card games and figuring-out games are most popular. Others, such as the miniature billiards and sports games with youngsters manipulating players on each team, have also become enormously popular. Many parents find these games more fun to play with their children than the ones mentioned earlier.

The Stanley Cup

Carolyn, nine, and George, seven, were playing with George's new ice hockey game. Each sat at one end of the table and turned knobs that moved the players forward and backward and swung their hockey sticks, moving the puck. Their father and the man who lived next door, Pat Snyder, were watching the Sunday afternoon football game on television in the same room. Carolyn had scored four goals, George none. George's face looked like a thundercloud. Even the family Persian cat, Ayatollah, took one look and hid under the couch.

George finally said, "It's my game. You can't play anymore."

Father: "Now, George, you've got to share it with your sister. If you don't, you won't have anybody to play with."

George: "I will, too! I'll get Joey from down the street."

Pat, Father's neighbor, said, "Listen, I think I know what's going wrong. That game depends on how fast you can twist the little levers that move the men and the sticks. You've got kids about two years apart playing that game. One of them is bound to be more coordinated than the other and she'll win all the time. Besides, it's George's game, and that rubs his nose in it even more."

Father: "What'll we do? Maybe we can give George a handicap. George, you're younger than Carolyn, how about starting out a couple of goals ahead? Carolyn, would that be okay with you?"

It was okay with Carolyn but not with George. He wanted to win from scratch or not play at all. To save face he said, "Aw, I don't like this game anyway. It's junk."

Carolyn exclaimed, "I think it's choice."

Father decided to put it aside for George and his age mates.

During a television commercial, Pat said, "You know, I found a solution to this problem by luck. I bought a game for my kids. It's like the Super Bowl, a football game where players move up and down the the field with the ball. But it's one of those electronic gadgets where you have to press buttons. You only have a *little* bit of control over the ball. The men take over once you've committed yourself to a play. It's funny how my kids, all those different ages, can play that game together and not be jealous of each other. They root for their team, but the thing seems to make them about evenly matched. So nobody gets too far ahead just because they're more advanced in using their hands, their eyes, and their brains. There's still a lot of luck as well as some strategy in it; your hockey game is almost all skill and strategy. And you know, at our house, they can blame something else besides themselves. It's the computer's fault. They holler at the lights that go on, the buttons that weren't fast enough, or what not."

Father says, "You know, I've noticed the same thing with the other presents we've given George, those little racing cars that go up and down the track. He can play that with his sister without losing his temper or falling apart. It's as if they each have a car that represents them, but then they cheer for the car and the *cars* are the competitors. They're one step removed. There isn't really much they can do about the race once it starts. They make a lot of noise winding up the cars to start with, but I don't know how much difference that really makes. Neither do they, so they seem to take losing easier. They can blame it on the cars."

You may buy a fancy electronic game with all sorts of cartridges with games that play on a television screen and find that your kids, after the initial excitement, rarely use it. That's because it depends on manual dexterity and one member of the family usually proves superior as time goes along. Practice helps. But often the one who practices the most is the most skilled. He or she plays alone (these games allow you to play against yourself) because the others have given up. Somehow the handicap button doesn't seem to click.

If you move from purely chance games that depend on luck to those that involve some skill as well, choose carefully. You don't need to invest in overpriced, overstimulating gadgets that always seem to come unassembled and without batteries. Simple games will do.

Probably the board games with competitive and cooperative elements are a useful step beyond this. Jigsaw puzzles also have the advantage of allowing for competition as well as cooperation. Look for games entailing some kind of "danger," such as being stranded in space or people who need to be rescued. Youngsters can often get together long enough to work out a strategy, to cooperate to achieve a worthwhile goal, especially if it's a scary situation! It draws them together. Games where players have to figure out how their play and strategy affects others probably teach reasoning the best.

Yahtzee, for which knowledge of odds is probably more important than the luck that seems so apparent (it's a dice game), is a good example. If one child is a lot younger than another, he or she would most likely have trouble keeping up.

In Clue, things have to be figured out by reasoning, by the process of elimination; it again depends on one's stage of development in thinking. Clue, chess, Scrabble, checkers, dominoes, Twenty Questions, and puzzles rely on strategy more than chance. But the old favorites still appeal the most.

The Kennedy family fed on good healthy competition. Jacqueline Kennedy Onassis said of them when she first joined the clan: "After dinner they all play guessing games like categories or charades or Twenty Questions—you're doing mental somersaults all the time." The parlor game of Monopoly was a great favorite of the Kennedys; they played it almost every night. When Jackie would get too bored, she would deliberately make a couple of mistakes to end the game. "Does Jack mind?" she was asked. "Not if I'm on the other side," she replied.*

Monopoly has been with us for generations. It combines chance and strategy. Its universal appeal survived the era of its birth. Perhaps collecting properties and building on them, owning railroads and utilities, dealing with fantastic sums of money are as appealing to adults as to children, maybe more so. It's a game that crosses age lines.

* Eleanor Harris, "The Senator Is in a Hurry," *McCall's*, August 1957.

Go Directly to Jail—and Stay There!

Sarah and Margie were very involved in a Monopoly game. Each was doing her own thing and it was fairly close. They hadn't even fought over whether the banker absconded with the funds or not! Usually in Monopoly the girls had been so involved that they didn't compare money, properties, and so forth. When they got stuck, they started comparing before the end of the game.

The chance cards, which usually gave everybody the same break and provided a note of suspense, were going against Margie. She was getting very frustrated trying to get out of jail and not being able to roll the right combination. Her tolerance had been reached. The game got stuck. The bickering began. Margie got angry at the chance cards and claimed they hadn't been shuffled enough.

Mother, hearing the commotion, said, "Margie, are you having a problem with your sister?"

Margie: "Not me—everyone does—they all hate her!"

Mother: "We'll have to put the game away if the two of you can't work it out."

Margie said, "I won't help put it away! Let her put it away!"

Sarah: "I won."

Margie: "No, you didn't! We didn't finish! Besides, you cheat! Yesterday in Clue you got Colonel Mustard in the Conservatory with the Rope on the second try. You must've peeked at the secret cards."

Sarah: "I did not!"

Mother: "Okay, let's leave the game for now the way it is. It's time to take a break. Everybody get a book or something quiet for a while. Maybe later I'll play you each a good game of checkers."

She had intervened and split them up. Before bedtime

she played checkers with each. Checkers also crosses age lines. You can keep improving and that's good. It's never hopeless, and playing with an adult often softens the intensity of the need to win. Margie said to her mother, "I like checkers better. You have more pieces, not just two, one against one, like in Monopoly."

Mother said, "Yes, maybe that does make a difference. Monopoly is very exciting with the safe places you can be and the ways you can set traps for the other person, but I notice sometimes you kids get too worked up. Maybe because it's one against one. Also, there are those huge, unreal amounts of money involved. Checkers is a good game for learning rules, isn't it?"

Unfortunately, Mother's question came at the wrong time. Margie had just moved a piece backward illegally.

Mother: "Are we playing by checkers rules or Margie's rules?"

Margie: "Checkers rules." She moved another piece backward.

Mother: "Margie, what would your sister do if you played that way with her?"

Margie: "She'd have a fit! But you're my mother."

Mother: "Well, I'm not going to have a fit, but if we're going to play cheating checkers, let's call it that. Every time you cheat, let's make up a cheating rule for it. And I'm allowed to cheat, too, if I make up a rule." Soon the two of them had so many cheating rules that they were laughing about the whole thing and Margie said, "Let's go back to the real rules. This is no fun."

Mother had successfully used the "paradox" (see the section "Using the Paradox" in Chapter III) and invented "cheating checkers." She'd given Margie plenty of rope instead of fighting with her about it. It worked.

In the Monopoly fiasco, Mother might have tried to get the girls to change roles. If they were willing, the winner could feel what it was like to be losing. And after all, it was only pretend, like Margie being stuck in jail and not being able to get out, and losing her turns. If she could just temporarily be relieved from that hot seat by changing roles with Sarah and Sarah could see what it was like, maybe playing could continue. Or at least it might not blow up next time.

Mother decided to set up a special space in a corner of the living room and called it the game corner. She put a table and cabinet there with all the games. There was no spare room in the house, but a space designated for games, a place where the kids knew they could be a little louder and rougher than in the rest of the living room, quieted things down. And perhaps the kids would agree to keep it neat and pick it up since it was theirs.

Through play, youngsters develop muscular ability, their minds, and imaginations, learn about the world around them, including its rules (and gradually learn to respect them). But as parents know, even school age youngsters in the Law and Order stage accept defeat—assuming that their opponents have played a fair and better game—much more easily with friends at school and in the neighborhood than with brothers and sisters.

Among brothers and sisters, the rules may be acknowledged, but they don't have to be strictly obeyed. Cheating is more frequent. Often fairness is forgotten. It becomes okay to win in any old way, using any means. They forget about struggling for victory within the rules of the game. Often they cheat if they don't think they have the ability to win fairly. Sadly, they usually have it but they're afraid to take a chance and find out. Cheating is really a no-win policy. Tell them they won't really be proud of a win by cheating because it's not a real victory. They'll always doubt their own ability if they make cheating a habit. There's no chance to gain self-confidence. Here, Mother played with Margie gently to help her realize by herself that she was cheating. She was cheating and then denying it. Just accusing her wouldn't do any good. She had to open up a discussion of it without being defensive and breaking up the game. That only ends in a huff. And of course, Mother later gave Margie lots of support and praise when she finally won a game fair and square. That's crucial.

Eventually your kids learn that even in the family competing without fighting and sticking to the rules is more fun than winning by cheating. This means they are getting ready for the adult world, where they'll need to compete for jobs and other roles in life—it's a time when the aggressiveness of childhood needs to be channeled constructively if you are going to win at all.

Working Mothers

The great controversy persists about whether mothers of small children can work and raise their families, too. Some think it's an either/or situation: either a woman stays home and raises her children or she postpones a family for a job and career. A generation ago most women began work (or returned to work) after their children had grown up so there really wasn't a controversy. But there were many exceptions.

Miss Lillian Carter quite candidly says, "I do believe in working women and I feel so strongly that a child is better off not to have the mother every minute of the time. Children who cling to their mothers—they grow up being babies. And I think it is good for a mother and a child to be separated most of the day."*

Maybe that's why her son, President Jimmy Carter, sometimes mends his own clothes and became famous for carrying his own garment bag on and off Air Force One. Children whose mothers work need to grow up and learn to take care of themselves early. Carter's mother worked as a nurse throughout his childhood. He described his memory of her working

* "Lillian Carter Talks About Racism, the Kennedys, and Jimmy's Reign," *Ms.*, October 1976.

almost all the time and, as he recalls it now, usually between twelve and twenty hours a day.*

Juanita Kreps, the former Secretary of Commerce and a model career woman admired by millions, doesn't share Lillian Carter's enthusiasm. She says, "I don't feel I'm giving my children . . . the day-to-day thoughtful attention they merit."† She was happy in her work, but says she paid a high price. So you can see there is a wide range of feeling about working among mothers.

In the past, most child-raising authorities felt that a mother should stay home with an infant for the first several years so that the youngster was pretty well along on the road to independence. During that time Mother is the protector and teacher about the world.

Breaking the strong close tie between a mother and an infant was taboo. In spite of this strong advice from mental health professionals, the number of working mothers has tripled in less than two decades. In 1970, less than 20 percent of mothers of preschool children were working; today almost two-thirds of wives with husbands who have small children are working.‡ The numbers are still on the rise. The reasons are economic (many women must work to support or help support the family); political (more opportunities for women to work are available); and psychological (it's now considered acceptable, sometimes even desirable, that women have a career outside the home. So for many it's important for their self-esteem). Whatever the reasons, it's happened. What new problems does this cause for the children, and how do they show up?

That Piece of Mommy Is Mine!

Jennifer Wilson worked as an administrative assistant in a large company. Her children were four and a half

* Carter, *Why Not the Best?*
† Associated Press, May 30, 1979.
‡ H. Hayghe, "Families and the Rise of Working Wives—An Overview," *Monthly Labor Review* 99 (1976).

and three. Jennifer worked because she wanted to. She had always worked, took two or three months' maternity leave to have each child, and then went back to her job. The children, Priscilla and Walter, were well cared for in a neighbor's home during the day.

It was a typical evening and Jennifer was cooking dinner. She liked to cook but her day was very crowded. So when she got home from one full-time job and had to switch gears to another full-time job, that of mother and housewife, she was tired. Her husband, George, usually helped, but he wasn't home from work yet. It was easier to make dinner if the kids were watching TV. But Priscilla wanted to help her mother at the kitchen counter, so she dragged over a stool and stood up on it. She loved being close to her mother. Pounding the hamburger into patties was fun, too.

Walter spotted her. He said, "I want to get up, too," and tried to climb on Priscilla's stool. He knocked her off. Zonk! She landed on her head. Soon she recovered and pushed over the stool Walter was perched on. As he was falling, he grabbed for Mommy. She cut her finger with the knife. She yelled, "You kids are just too much! There's no way I can cut myself in half for you! I have to make the dinner. That comes first right now. So scram, go watch TV."

But both children just sat on the floor crying. They'd been watching television all afternoon. Their memories of Mommy were all about her leaving every morning. In the evening they wanted her. But now they had to compete with dinner. It wasn't fair. Walter: "I'll be good, Mommy. Can I come up and help?"

Her heart melted because she'd been missing them all day, too. Mother: "Okay, let's get another stool. Priscilla, you get up on this side, and, Walter, you on this side. Priscilla, you work with the hamburger. Walter, you see if you can open this box of peas." (Later) "You know, it really is more fun when the three of us do it together."

Jennifer Wilson and George, her husband, had read about latchkey children, children of the sweatshop days in England when women *had* to work. Young children got a large ring around their neck with a latchkey on it so they could let themselves into the house. But the main problem was that they had to take care of themselves. They had to grow up too fast into the adult world, lonely and frightened, never really experiencing childhood.

The Wilsons didn't want their youngsters to be like this. They knew that today's latchkey children watch television all afternoon, averaging seven or eight hours of television viewing a day. There's nothing else for them to do. Jennifer had a friend who worked and was so pressed for time to spend with her children she even kept them up late at night watching television with her. The late shows, of course, are adult movies. So Jennifer was determined to be different.

She told George: "I think I really spend more time with the kids in the evening and weekends than my friends who don't work. Somehow those times are precious for me. I guess that's why we don't go out so much."

George: "No question about it, the fact that both of us work gets me more involved in taking care of the kids than my friends whose wives don't work. I like it. Tomorrow's Saturday and my day to take Walter and Priscilla to McDonald's for breakfast. They're really having fun learning how to eat out. And you can sleep late."

Jennifer: "I appreciate that, honey. But the kids keep asking what I do at work. It must be pretty mysterious for them. Maybe it makes them even madder to have to share me with each other *and* with some 'dumb old office.' I know what; I'm going to bring them to the office some morning next week. They can look around and see my desk and leave some notes and messages on the bulletin board for me. I really want them to feel good about my working, because I do. I don't think I could have been a full-time mother. I'm just not that type. But sometimes I do feel guilty about it, even though I don't put the job ahead of them. The kids and my work are both important. They both make me feel good, just like being married to you does, George. And I think it's good for them to deal with all kinds of people—other kids, teachers, and the baby-sitter. I get exasperated when I come home and they climb all over me and pull on me, but I guess I'd be pretty hurt if they didn't. It would mean something was wrong, and they didn't care one way or the other. But I still worry about them during the day."

George, laughing: "Maybe we ought to get a beeper like doctors and maintenance people carry. Then they could beep you anytime they needed you and you wouldn't have to worry about not being in touch."

Jennifer: "That's not as silly as it sounds. But I think things are working out pretty well for us. Well, it's time for their bed, and I promised them each an extra story tonight. But I've only got two hands. Maybe I'll read it to them together."

George: "No, we've agreed to give them individual attention around bedtime. Your turn for Priscilla. I'll take Walter."

Jennifer and George knew that the quality of time spent with children is as important, if not more important, than the quantity. And they didn't try to make up for absences by showering their children with toys and presents. They planned things well. Jennifer had made sure that her job had consistent hours. She'd turned down a higher paying job with longer and less predictable hours. It was important for the children to know exactly when she'd be home and have it the same, day after day. She'd chosen the baby-sitter *very* carefully after interviewing several. She knew that the person's style should be as close to hers as she could find. She hadn't switched one to another, because the kids needed continuity with another person who would fill in for Mother during work hours.

Jennifer realized it was a stress for kids not to be alone with their mothers for the first year or so. But stress is a part of life and even at that tender age can be compensated for. There wasn't any point in her staying home when she wouldn't have been satisfied or happy being a full-time mother. It would've made things worse on herself *and* the children.

Sure, it was hard to crowd so much into a twenty-four-hour day. The children fought over her because their time with her was so limited. In a way that was reassuring. They switched from the baby-sitter to her with eagerness, so she wasn't afraid of being replaced by somebody else in their hearts. She really believed the children fought less with each other because they had grown up knowing several adults who took care of them. She wasn't the *only* one to fight over and get attention from. They could switch off, from herself, to their father, their grandmother who lived nearby, and the neighbor–baby-sitter.

Still, Jennifer worried about their grade school years coming up. She didn't want them to be latchkey children. She knew that clubs, lessons, and visiting friends weren't the right answers for after school. She was determined to lobby at the elementary school for after-school recreation programs organized for children of working mothers. There had to be regular hours and supervision. This would otherwise be an empty part of the day and perhaps a more vulnerable period for them than their time now spent with a carefully selected sitter.

Jennifer had looked at a day care center but hadn't been happy with the ratio of staff to children. She wanted a ratio of one to four because she felt that young, preschool children should have this much adult attention. Maybe the day care center movement needed some lobbying, too, if it was going to improve in their community. Things were going well for Jennifer and her family. Part of the reason was that she liked her work. She didn't work just because she had to.

New opportunities for women, and new viewpoints about their working, have changed child-rearing practices drastically. There's no question that it's a real stress for young children when Mother returns to work. The young child would prefer to be with her. If she prefers to be with the children she should stay home, unless, of course, economic considerations force her to work. Women have proved it can be done without terrible consequences.

The easiest time to leave home for work is when your children have started school or preschool. In school they have their own separate lives. Before that their whole life is wrapped up with you. If you go to work before they start preschool it's probably best to do it when they're babies. That sounds strange. But after three months they're beginning to depend on you more and more if you're the only or main one who takes care of them. Interrupting (and disrupting) the very close mother-child tie that begins to develop between three and six months and goes on until the second or third year is asking for trouble. Try to avoid starting work during this time (from six months to two and a half years) if possible.

Within that time frame, the period between ten and fifteen months is most crucial not to disrupt. It is the practicing stage discussed earlier. Children are "practicing" going away and coming back to mother—being on their own for short periods. They need to do it cautiously, at their own pace. They won't understand if you suddenly are away for most of the day during the middle of that trying-out period. What will they do? Well, they'll probably get discouraged and afraid to take chances. And they'll be mad as well as frightened. Who better to take out being mad on than a brother or sister, especially a baby who comes along later?

So, you see, the *timing* of going back to work can affect sibling rivalry. You don't want to do anything to make it worse than it normally is, do you? The stage can be set early for growing up through the first and second years of life with two "mothers"—you, the real one, and another one represented by a reliable, consistent relative or hired sitter who should be very carefully chosen, or a small day care center that pays attention to the emotional needs of children. Then the child can "practice" with several people, apparently without harm.

Yes, it's possible to have a career and a family at the same time and not put one ahead of the other. It's done all the time. They are *different*. Neither the joys nor the sorrows are the same. For many women, combining the two makes for a fuller and richer life. It's not either/or. Both can work together to complement and supplement each other. A mother who works brings a sense of accomplishment and organization home with her—and a special sensitivity toward people to work with her. There are problems. But they can be minimized with careful planning by both parents, and sharing in the care of the youngsters, as Jennifer and George did.

The Single-Parent Family

America's spiraling divorce rate is not news. One-half of all marriages now end in divorce. On the average, they last six or seven years. So young children are primarily affected. Between 20 and 25 percent of *all* children will experience the divorce of their parents before they finish their school years. And according to the U.S. Census Bureau, half of the kids being born today will live a good part of their lives with a single parent.

The single-parent family has become a statistical norm in our country. It's no longer just an "alternate family style." Single-parent families are growing at three times the rate of dual-parent families. Many special problems are associated with them, and many of the effects on children (particularly long-term effects) are still unknown. One thing is certain. The loss of the partnership and half the parent pair, and the stress on the custodial parent to make up for it, demands a redistribution of roles and functions among the remaining family members. And the first few months are the hardest.

Adjustment to divorce is more difficult for an only child. Brother-and-sister units generally remain intact when parents separate and divorce; *they* aren't split up. So they have each other. This means that often parents note a *lessening* of sibling rivalry after divorce because of the children's need to stick together and support each other. Curiously, after divorce rivalry can get better *or* worse.

Special problems that affect the brother-and-sister unit seriously and show up in a *worsening* of their relationship are directly or indirectly related to the divorce experience itself. Let's look at two examples of how and why fighting may get worse. The first deals with the loss of one parent and the competition between the siblings to take that parent's place. The second is related to the children's loyalty and conflicts over the parents who have split up. First, let's look at what happens to family roles when someone leaves.

The Man of the House

Karen Black was stunned by the divorce. Her husband had just walked out. Suddenly, the world seemed frightening. She was overwhelmed by the emotional job of taking care of two sons, David, eight, and Fred, six. Without much money, she was having trouble just making ends meet. Running the household alone was too much. So the sudden increase in the boys' fighting threw her for a loop. She felt as if caught in a revolving door, trying to break up fights all day.

"Will you boys stop wrestling? Now you've broken the coffee table! I'm fed up to here!"

Fred: "Well, he wanted to tell me I couldn't go roller skating. Who's he? The boss? I can decide things around here, too! And tell him to stop twisting my arm."

Mother: "Ever since daddy left you guys have been fighting to see who's the new man of the house—to decide who can boss who around. You never fought like this before, at least not so violently. It isn't just wrestling anymore. What's wrong?"

David: "Well, you're different—you seem scared and don't know what to do anymore. So we're toughening ourselves up. Besides, Dad isn't here anymore to stop us before someone gets hurt."

Mother: "Yes, I guess he did keep the lid on. Now each of you wants to fill in the gap to make us a whole family again. We just can't be the same. I'm mad at him for leaving us and so are you. This isn't the way to get over it, letting all that anger break through with each other. It's tough without a father, but I'm not going to let you guys fight over his job. It'll be awhile till I really feel okay again; for now, we're going to set up some new rules—about fighting, especially. So people can live peaceably togther."

Often when Goliath leaves the house, the "Davids" try to take over being the "man of the house."* Because one important peacekeeping factor is suddenly missing there may be an upsurge of intense fighting between the kids while the home is unsettled and new ways of living (and getting along reasonably well) have been set up. The oldest may try to become the disciplinarian and punish the younger. But he's in no shape to become the father. Mother may be paralyzed for a while but she'll recover. She doesn't need to declare martial law. Just firm limits and controls will do. So things can begin to get back on track again. So people can learn to live and let live. And there's more and more help available in the

* Kay Tooley, "Antisocial behavior and social alienation post divorce: The 'Man of the House' and his mother," *American Journal of Orthopsychiatry* 46 (1): 33–42. 1976.

community for families who are divorcing, as you'll see in the next example.

It's the natural tendency of children to wonder who was "at fault" after a divorce. In their own fighting, parents have usually blamed each other for problems in the marriage, so it's natural for the children to do the same and take different sides.

You Can't Make the Pill Retroactive

Amy Rutherford knew the divorce was coming. She'd felt the slow deterioration in the marriage, the increased irritability and arguments, intensifying later into fights and ending in the decision to separate. The children, Roy, seven, and Ruth, five, knew something was wrong but they were shocked when Daddy moved out. The first twelve months were very difficult. Everyone was upset; Mother had to go back to work. That wasn't so bad because she had worked before and could get a good job. So it wasn't new for her or the kids.

But Ruth, who had been learning to read in school, stopped learning. She just sat there daydreaming. She thought to herself, *If they were going to get divorced, why did they have us in the first place?* She was angry and unhappy. So was Roy. Roy and Ruth began arguing more.

Roy: "Mommy's too strict with us. All she does is yell and holler. I wish I lived with Dad."

Ruth: "Daddy's the bad one. I heard Mommy say that he's not paying the money to take care of us. He doesn't care about us. Or why would he leave us?"

Roy: "Shut up, you don't know anything! What about Mommy and her boy friend? That's not being very loyal to Dad."

Ruth: "But Daddy *doesn't* care about us. He didn't even come by to pick us up last Sunday. I hate him! He's like Darth Vader." (Darth Vader, a *Star Wars* character, was once the strongest and noblest of the Jedi knights. But he turned evil and became a dark, hulking, dangerous figure. And Ruth had once loved her daddy very much. He could do no wrong—until he left home. He had turned on them.)

Roy: "But he gives us things and takes us places. Look at the toys he gives us."

Ruth: "I hate my presents. A fur skunk. What kind of a present is that? I hate the ones he gave you, too. I'm going to break them all."

Roy: "You're stupid! You don't know anything. Dad lets us stay up late when we stay over at his apartment and Mom makes us go to bed at eight o'clock. Nobody else in the *world* has to go to bed at eight o'clock!"

Amy overhears the children's argument and it hurts her very much. Basically she feels as Ruth does. She thinks to herself, *If their daddy wants to play Santa Claus every Sunday afternoon, that's his business. "Disneyland Daddy"—always taking them on a fun trip or vacation and making up for the time he never gave them with all those presents. It's not fair! Why doesn't he spend a Sunday afternoon over here and help me wash the windows? He's the lucky one. Anybody can stand the noise and the mess of taking care of two kids for a Sunday afternoon. You know it's going to be over in a few hours. I've got it all week long.*

In spite of these thoughts, Amy had recently had two appointments at the divorce counseling clinic and learned a great deal about children's reactions to divorce, the stages they go through, and her responses as well. She decided to stop battling with her husband over visitation. The battles seemed artificial anyway, as if she kept them going so she wouldn't have to sit alone and helpless. She was so frightened of being lonely.

Her former husband had agreed to go with her for the

next clinic appointment when she told him about it. It would be set up to work on "co-parenting." The idea was, they told her at the clinic, that children badly need access to both parents. Parents need to try to restore as much continuity to the children's lives as possible now that the partnership between them wasn't a daily one. They needed to take turns and spell each other, like a relay team, so one parent was always available. Responsibilities should be divided up so that one parent didn't get all the heavy stuff and the other all the fun. They would try to decide who would be responsible for taking the kids to doctor's appointments, who'd take them to athletic events, who'd take them to music lessons, who would attend PTA meetings.

Amy felt there was hope, that they were getting back on the right track. She could handle things much better once they got started dividing up the parenting tasks and had negotiated a co-parenting agreement. The kids had been feeling the effects of their disagreements and were reverberating under them in a natural way.

Instead of shouting at the children to stop fighting or taking it out on Roy because he was on his father's side, she decided to try to reunite the children. After all, she'd learned that they needed their relationship strengthened; it was a healthy part of the family that hadn't been fragmented. Right now it was reflecting the divorce tensions, the breaking up of the husband and wife team. She would try to reverse that.

"Kids, I know it's hard," she told them. "It's hard on me and I know it's hard on you. The idea that Daddy or I is to blame is the most likely conclusion for you to come to. It's the way kids think anyway, and I guess it's the way we've acted. When you kids get into a fight with each other or with other kids, it's natural to consider the other guy at fault. I've never heard anybody say, 'I started it!' And if you think everyone is either good or bad, guilty or innocent, it's natural you'd think about your parents the same way. One, the good guy, and the other, the bad guy.

"It really isn't that way. I think your Dad would say the same thing. There's good and bad in each of us. People aren't all good or all bad. Your Dad and I are working on that and I think you're going to find a difference in us. He won't be quizzing you about whether I'm dating anybody, and I won't be asking you to give him messages about his payments every month. We've agreed to keep you guys out of it."

Divorce ends the role spouses have with each other. They usually don't like to think about the reality that it doesn't end their role and responsibilities as parents.

The "parenting" part of them can become paralyzed for a while, usually for the first six to eighteen months after the divorce. Realignments are forged within the family. Often the oldest child assumes the role of the absent parent, with more responsibility suddenly placed on him or her. Economic disruption forces most mothers to go back to work or to start work for the first time, which is even harder.

As I've mentioned, the only child is probably more at risk than several siblings are. Brothers and sisters have each other, but the only child is adrift all alone. He or she may have to grow up fast and learn how to be an adult companion for the parent, who often out of loneliness and loss focuses more intensely on the youngster than before.

With several children, the problems are different. Fortunately, Amy recognized that the loyalty conflicts and taking sides (which caused more and more trouble between Roy and Ruth) musn't be reinforced. They should be reversed, and she'd taken steps to do just that. She's identified the cause— the natural tendency of kids to blame, to divide people into good and bad, reinforced by the actual behavior of a divorcing couple. And she's reassured them that it isn't true. And she'll show them from now on.

Now that the *event* of the divorce is over, the process of life goes on. Amy wants to prevent the later difficulties that she has seen her friends experience—mothers who can't manage their adolescent sons' behavior, children who grow up only to marry and divorce over and over, as if searching for a solution, but unable to draw on the right experience from early life to make it work.

Amy will also talk more frankly with the children about the divorce itself, the reasons for it, the problems around it, and how they're being resolved. She'll include the children in her discussion with her husband about a parenting agreement. She'll share it with them. Most of all, she wants them to have each other again as friends, for their relationship as brother and sister is probably what they'll remember best later on. Indeed, it may be one of the most important factors in determining how they'll turn out.

Finally, let's consider a problem that's not unique to single-parent families, but often becomes exaggerated.

What Happened? Tell Me All About It

Derek had custody of his two children, Mark, five, and Lisa, three. When he came home at night from work, he was tired. He sat down with a beer and the newspaper. His mother, who lived with them now that he was divorced, told him the children had been fighting all day: "Mark was awful! He bullied her and broke her doll. I don't know what to do about that boy!" Derek took Mark up on his lap. He wanted to be an understanding father. "Mark, tell me what happened, tell me all about it."

Mark: "Lisa won't stay out of my room. She broke my train."

Father: "Lisa, come on up here, honey. Now why did you do that?"

Lisa: "He squirted me with his squirt gun, and he got my dollies all wet."

Derek hugs them both with each arm. There are tears in his eyes. "You kids ought to get along better. How about it? Will you promise to be good tomorrow? For Daddy? You know how much he loves you both."

"Sure, Daddy."

You can imagine how long that promise will last—probably for ten minutes after Daddy goes to work the next day. Then they'll be at each other again. Because it's the only way to get Daddy's attention. If they're good, they don't get to sit on his lap in the evening, only if they've fought. And it's so warm and snuggly up there. Especially now that Mommy isn't around much. Daddy seems to be interested in them the most when they fight. So they'll keep it up as long as he rewards it. Of course, he doesn't know he's reinforcing their fighting—not for a while at least.

Soon it began to dawn on him what he was doing. He made a conscious effort to change. He took them in his lap and read a story every evening without asking if they'd been good that day. He voiced disapproval of their fighting, but didn't try to figure it out with them because they were too young to know who started what. By the time he came home they had forgotten anyway. Derek told Grandmother to handle it when it happened during the day. All she needed was permission and authority to do so. She'd raised children of her own.

So give your children the attention they need. Just as they need their vitamins every day, they need their emotional vitamins, too. Don't let them associate caring with fighting, or they'll give you more of what gets them their vitamins.

Jane and Peter Fonda are each very talented and successful artists in their own right. And their father, Henry Fonda, before them. They didn't achieve it easily. Their mother and father separated when they were young. According to *Jane,**

* Thomas Kiernan, *Jane* (New York: G. P. Putnam's Sons, 1973).

an unofficial biography, Peter was jealous of the attention Jane got from their father. It didn't matter if it was scolding. He'd rather have had that than nothing. According to the story, he acted up and his problem behavior drew his father's attention. At least it was better than indifference. While Henry Fonda was out of the country on a honeymoon with his new wife, a lonely and unhappy Peter accidentally shot himself. His father rushed home to his side. If that's how it happened, it's a tough way to have to use to get attention.

Peter and Jane each grew up to become an accomplished and fulfilled person. It wasn't easy. You can make it easier for your children.

CONCLUSION—

The Myths and the Realities

Perhaps the best way to conclude is to recap some of the main points I've explained in this book. They're mostly common misconceptions that puzzle and confuse parents, the common myths of sibling rivalry. Here they are in shorthand:

1. Myth: Brothers and sisters should naturally love each other.

   Reality: Maybe they should, but they don't. When they're young, they're naturally selfish. Everybody wants to be boss; each wants *more* than the other—more toys, more desserts, and more of you. They want to be first, number one. It's not very attractive, but that's the way it is for some time. It's the number one gripe of parents in this country.

2. Myth: Everyone else's children get along so well.

   Reality: It only seems that way. As parents, we're overinvolved with our own kids. They're an extension of ourselves; when they're hurt, it feels as if it's happening to us. That's why we exaggerate the fighting of our own kids. It's embarrassing to us. We minimize it in other families.

3. Myth: Let them fight it out. It's a good safety valve for anger, steam to be let off.

Reality: Jealousy and envy between brothers and sisters
             for parents' affection is indeed very normal. But
             it's one thing to *feel* it and another thing to *act*
             on it by beating one another to a pulp. No child
             has ever been harmed by being helped to control
             angry and jealous feelings.

4. Myth: Children no longer accept parents' authority.
             We need a new approach. The family should
             be considered a democracy with everyone equal.

   Reality: The family is, in fact, not a democracy. At best,
             it's a *guided* democracy. The family really is a
             situation of unequal power, both between the
             children themselves and between the parents
             and children. Like it or not, parents are the
             authority. It's their job to see that this authority
             is used responsibly.

5. Myth: They'd stop fighting if I could treat them all
             equally.

   Reality: It makes no sense to treat them all equally be-
             cause they're all different: physically, in age,
             and emotionally. You like them for different
             reasons and when you dislike them it's for dif-
             ferent reasons. The most important thing is to
             try to be *fair*.

6. Myth: Brothers and sisters will be reasonable with each
             other if only you spend enough time reasoning
             with them.

   Reality: Young children operate with the very simple
             attitude that might equals right, both between
             themselves and their parents. You have to deal
             with them at this level, but at the same time
             help them grow beyond it into reasonableness.
             It's one of the main jobs of good parenting.

7. Myth: You should begin to teach children to share
              with each other from the very beginning.

    Reality: Young children are just naturally selfish and
              grow out of it slowly. Before they'll give up some
              of their selfishness, they need to feel secure
              about themselves. Even then, everyone should
              have the right to hold onto *some* individuality;
              children shouldn't have to share *everything* (un-
              less you're bringing them up to live in a people's
              commune).

8. Myth: But I want them to grow up being friends.
              Maybe I can teach them to share by repeating
              the idea over and over again.

    Reality: You can't teach them to share by sheer deter-
              mination any more than you can just stamp out
              jealousy. Strange as it may seem, if you try to
              promote sharing too early, you'll tend to trigger
              even more selfishness and the stage will last
              longer. Trying to make them friends, with the
              best of all intentions, often boomerangs. Stress
              their own individuality and the friendship will
              most likely develop by itself.

9. Myth: I try to get my kids to imitate each *other's* good
              habits by pointing them out.

    Reality: "Look how well Susie eats" and "How neat
              Johnny keeps his room" sound so tempting, but
              those well-meant messages invariably backfire.
              There's plenty of natural competition between
              them already. Don't reinforce it. If you do, you'll
              be *rewarding* their rivalry and increasing it with-
              out even knowing. They'll apply your compari-
              sons as standards to exaggerate differences be-
              tween them. And the resentments will build.

10. Myth: Christmas is a time when kids get so many

things they want, they forget about fighting. And it teaches them the rewards of "being good" during the year.

Reality: Unfortunately kids never really seem to be satisfied—at least not for long. In fact, they can be overstimulated by too many presents. So pick them carefully. At Christmas, kids can be more touchy than ever because often the expectations for "being good" are too great and last too long so they can't meet them. And the pressure on you for making sure everyone is happy can build up until you become a walking nervous break-down. So relax. Allow for a little increased irritability in you and them.

11. Myth: Fighting between brothers and sisters is the same now as it was twenty years ago.

Reality: It's probably somewhat more intense now because family size has changed. In families with four or five children, it was spread around by sheer numbers. Each child served as a buffer for the others. Now, in a typical family of just two children, there's bound to be more struggling because they spend more time rubbing against each other.

12. Myth: There's less rivalry if children are close together in age—they have to learn teamwork.

Reality: Children only a year or two apart in age experience more *intense* interaction. It's probably best to space children two or three years apart so they experience enough separateness from each other and needn't constantly have to fight for their individuality.

13. Myth: Having an only child is the best way to avoid the problem completely.

Reality: Yes, it avoids the problem. But you pay a price for the peace and quiet of an only child. The only child may have more trouble learning the give-and-take of everyday life and often needs extra help learning to deal with other children.

14. Myth: When we become parents, we start with a clean slate. If we mess up raising our children, it's our own fault.

Reality: You probably never think about it, but your position in the family you grew up in—as an only, first, second, or third child—affects your role as a parent in important ways. For example, preferences or dislikes may be based on subtle similarities to your own brothers and sisters or even yourself.

15. Myth: Women should have either a career or children, not both.

Reality: If you took a vote, kids would prefer mothers to be at home with them—no question. But some women aren't happy or fulfilled as full-time mothers. For them, it's best to work and be mothers too. And many mothers must work for economic reasons. It doesn't lead to more fighting between the kids if it's carefully planned with good consistent auxiliary parenting introduced early. The experience of many mothers over the years has proven this.

16. Myth: It's best to take a year off to have a baby and then go back to work.

Reality: That can lead to one of the worst times to leave your baby: in the middle of a love affair with you. If you possibly can, plan to go back to work at one of two times: when your child has started preschool or elementary school or when the baby has settled down after the first few weeks or months. Try not to start work when your baby is between six months and two years old if you can help it. The really critical period is ten to fifteen months. It's a time when your child is most vulnerable to an abrupt change in time spent with you.

17. Myth: The oldest child has an advantage because he or she learns responsibility early—helping the parents raise the other children.

   Reality: There is a certain "advantage" for the oldest child. Often the oldest is closest to the parents. They often have higher expectations for the oldest. But problems can arise from the tendency to cast the oldest child as a "third parent"—with more responsibility for raising the others. The oldest needs most to be one of the siblings, not one of the parents.

18. Myth: Most young children aren't old enough to care much when a new baby is born into the family.

   Reality: Good preparation for a new baby is a crucial need for all children. Believe it or not, the amount of future fighting in your family may depend on how this period is handled. It's such a critical time because of the child's increased sensitivity about the parents' attitudes and the need to share them with the new baby.

19. Myth: Sibling rivalry is worse in single-parent families.

   Reality: Sometimes, after divorce, sibling rivalry can *improve* because the kids have a greater need to stick together and keep the sibling bond intact. But two special kinds of rivalry can appear—one is triggered by loyalty conflicts and children siding with one parent against the other. And the other happens when the kids fight harder to see who can take the place of the absent parent—to see who is boss. Everyone is in shock for a while, but new family relationships need to be established—ones that are realistic and allow people to live reasonably peacefully together.

20. Myth: Be consistent. Always treat fighting the same way.

Reality: Consistency is a virtue but not when it becomes a rigid policy. Children go through stages and their fights aren't just single events. It's part of a process, always changing. You need to know what the stages are and how to deal with your children differently as they move through them.

21. Myth: Don't encourage bargaining for favors between your kids. It'll make blackmail and bribery part of their character.

Reality: "You scratch my back and I'll scratch yours" is a temporary stage children go through. It's the first step beyond physical solutions for settling differences. So don't be afraid to encourage trade-offs between them: ("She won't go in your room if you don't go in hers"). Eventually it leads to a feeling of trust: that if you do things for other people, you'll get a return on your investment. Besides, it's a relief from the fighting.

22. Myth: Disapprove of fighting, but not the children themselves ("Of course we love you both; it's your behavior we don't like").

Reality: Usually you can't separate the two. There's nothing wrong with children feeling guilty when they fight. It gives them motivation to change.

If you only disapprove of the behavior, it gives them an excuse to use the rest of their lives ("It's not my fault" or "I couldn't help it").

23. Myth: Discipline for fighting should be restricted to taking away whatever they fight over.

    Reality: If removing the cause of the fighting doesn't work, it's important to have other forms of discipline available. Don't rely on one form only. Have a mixed bag. Isolation, for example. Children can learn that they have to stay in their rooms alone until they've cooled off and are fit for human company again.

24. Myth: Never use spanking. It's permanently harmful.

    Reality: Don't spank when you've completely lost your temper. But spanking, if controlled and *not used as the first form* of discipline, isn't necessarily harmful. Most parents find they need it at some time or another. Many parents love their children and use spanking; many *don't* love them and never spank. They use humiliation, which is worse. The most important thing for a child is to be loved, to be wanted. Everything else comes second.

25. Myth: Watching television is a good safety valve for blowing off steam and reduces fighting between the children. They get it out of their system by watching.

    Reality: We used to think that way. But more and more evidence suggests that television violence seems to stimulate and sometimes even teach fighting. For example, it teaches that it's okay for the good guys to use violence and that almost all problems between people can be solved in thirty or sixty minutes. So don't be afraid to censor and limit television watching for your children.

26. Myth: Getting involved in fighting only makes it worse. If I ignore it and let them alone, they'll settle things themselves.

Reality: Young children first need an adult to settle things for them; later they need an adult to help them find partial solutions by themselves; still later to let them settle things themselves. Don't feel guilty about intervening. They aren't born with the ability to settle conflicts.

27. Myth: Order games and toys from special catalogs because toy manufacturers have studied the problems of competition and know best how to minimize them.

Reality: Look over games and toys carefully *yourself* before you buy, and remember—some can make rivalry worse; others help neutralize it. Games may make conflicts worse if motor coordination, planning strategy, or mathematical ability give an unfair advantage to one child over another. Consider how much "luck" is a factor in the games you pick. You're the best judge, not a catalog. It doesn't know your kids.

28. Myth: There are no good guidelines for dealing with sibling rivalry. Just react to it the way you feel.

Reality: Families are all different and there are no packaged formulas. But many techniques can be tried to bring the real reasons for it in the open, to clarify and isolate them, and to begin to solve specific problems. Trying several methods described in this book may help you find out what works and what doesn't work for you—so you can develop your own style and find the approach that fits your family best.

A PERSONAL
POSTSCRIPT

I've told in the Foreword how this book began with the problem of buying gifts for my own children in an airport shop and the discovery that there was no book written for parents about sibling rivalry. Yet, as a practicing physician and a practicing parent of two young children, I knew there was no problem that puzzles us more.

Like all parents, Sally and I have a string of sibling rivalry stories to tell about the years when our kids were small. It's like bringing out their pictures to show. Except they always look so well behaved in the pictures!

We'll never forget the summer we drove our toddler and infant to Cape Cod to visit their Gramps and Nana. Of course, Baby John got lots and lots of attention. Grandparents always think babies are cute. Finally, his sister Beth decided she'd make him *really* cute. It was midafternoon. The two of them were so quiet, taking a beautiful nap we thought. Until we peeked in the window to check. She was decorating him from head to toe with Nana's bright red lipstick. Gramps said it was Indian war paint, but he could have passed for the tattooed boy in the circus. Just enough to make us laugh, especially since Gramps enjoyed it so much. But it reminded me of an episode he hadn't thought was so funny many years before, something much less diplomatic. Two of his sons, fed up with the youngest and what they thought was his favored role in the family, poured glue in his cap and firmly attached his shoes to the floor! But I guess when we're grandparents, it's time to be more relaxed. It's when we're *parents* we get so uptight because we feel responsible. Maybe a mixture of the two generations would be just the right temperament to deal with sibling problems.

Anyhow, Beth and John grew up and are now teenagers. We've seen lots of problems come and go—the arguments over television, bickering at the dinner table, in the car on long trips, while playing Monopoly . . . and the birthday parties that ended in tears. We made mistakes like all parents. And we know we were lucky, too. Most of all, we learned—you have to settle problems for them when they're young and gradually teach them to settle problems themselves as they grow older.

A fine line, to be sure. The main point is you've got to have the capacity for doing *both*—taking over *and* letting go. One just isn't enough. If you watch and listen carefully, you can tell if you've gone too far one way or the other.

The other night, one of our youngsters was getting a pound and a half of flesh by watching every last credit of a television program. The idea was to delay changing to the other's program as long as possible. Soon they were hollering at each other. When we came in, we couldn't solve anything. But just being there stopped the fight from escalating. As they agreed: "It's okay to stop us from fighting but that's not enough. It may look as if the fight is over but it's really only gone underground for a few minutes until you go away. It really doesn't change the way we *feel*. We have to work that out ourselves."

They're right—and we stay out of it now as much as we can. Because with teenagers, parents are bound to be wrong, five times out of four anyway!